Jesus: A Very Short Introduction

VERY SHORT INTRODUCTIONS are for anyone wanting a stimulating and accessible way into a new subject. They are written by experts, and have been translated into more than 45 different languages.

The series began in 1995, and now covers a wide variety of topics in every discipline. The VSI library now contains over 500 volumes—a Very Short Introduction to everything from Psychology and Philosophy of Science to American History and Relativity—and continues to grow in every subject area.

Titles in the series include the following:

AFRICAN HISTORY John Parker and
  Richard Rathbone
AGEING Nancy A. Pachana
ALGEBRA Peter M. Higgins
AMERICAN HISTORY Paul S. Boyer
AMERICAN IMMIGRATION
  David A. Gerber
AMERICAN LEGAL HISTORY
  G. Edward White
AMERICAN POLITICAL HISTORY
  Donald Critchlow
AMERICAN POLITICAL PARTIES
  AND ELECTIONS L. Sandy Maisel
AMERICAN POLITICS
  Richard M. Valelly
THE AMERICAN PRESIDENCY
  Charles O. Jones
AMERICAN SLAVERY
  Heather Andrea Williams
ANARCHISM Colin Ward
ANCIENT EGYPT Ian Shaw
ANCIENT GREECE Paul Cartledge
THE ANCIENT NEAR EAST
  Amanda H. Podany
ANCIENT PHILOSOPHY Julia Annas
ANCIENT WARFARE Harry Sidebottom
ANGLICANISM Mark Chapman
THE ANGLO-SAXON AGE John Blair
ANIMAL BEHAVIOUR
  Tristram D. Wyatt
ANIMAL RIGHTS David DeGrazia
ANXIETY Daniel Freeman and
  Jason Freeman
ARCHAEOLOGY Paul Bahn

ARISTOTLE Jonathan Barnes
ART HISTORY Dana Arnold
ART THEORY Cynthia Freeland
ASTROPHYSICS James Binney
ATHEISM Julian Baggini
THE ATMOSPHERE Paul I. Palmer
AUGUSTINE Henry Chadwick
BACTERIA Sebastian G. B. Amyes
BARTHES Jonathan Culler
BEAUTY Roger Scruton
THE BIBLE John Riches
BLACK HOLES Katherine Blundell
BLOOD Chris Cooper
THE BRAIN Michael O'Shea
THE BRICS Andrew F. Cooper
BRITISH POLITICS Anthony Wright
BUDDHA Michael Carrithers
BUDDHISM Damien Keown
BUDDHIST ETHICS Damien Keown
BYZANTIUM Peter Sarris
CANCER Nicholas James
CAPITALISM James Fulcher
CATHOLICISM Gerald O'Collins
THE CELTS Barry Cunliffe
CHEMISTRY Peter Atkins
CHOICE THEORY Michael Allingham
CHRISTIANITY Linda Woodhead
CIRCADIAN RHYTHMS Russell Foster
  and Leon Kreitzman
CITIZENSHIP Richard Bellamy
CLASSICAL MYTHOLOGY
  Helen Morales
CLASSICS Mary Beard and
  John Henderson

CLIMATE Mark Maslin
CLIMATE CHANGE Mark Maslin
THE COLD WAR Robert McMahon
COMBINATORICS Robin Wilson
COMMUNISM Leslie Holmes
COMPUTER SCIENCE Subrata Dasgupta
CONSCIOUSNESS Susan Blackmore
CONTEMPORARY ART
    Julian Stallabrass
CORAL REEFS Charles Sheppard
COSMOLOGY Peter Coles
THE CRUSADES Christopher Tyerman
DADA AND SURREALISM
    David Hopkins
DANTE Peter Hainsworth and
    David Robey
DARWIN Jonathan Howard
THE DEAD SEA SCROLLS
    Timothy Lim
DECOLONIZATION Dane Kennedy
DEMOCRACY Bernard Crick
DESIGN John Heskett
DINOSAURS David Norman
DREAMING J. Allan Hobson
DRUGS Les Iversen
DRUIDS Barry Cunliffe
THE EARTH Martin Redfern
ECONOMICS Partha Dasgupta
EGYPTIAN MYTH Geraldine Pinch
THE ELEMENTS Philip Ball
EMOTION Dylan Evans
EMPIRE Stephen Howe
ENGLISH LITERATURE Jonathan Bate
THE ENLIGHTENMENT
    John Robertson
EPICUREANISM Catherine Wilson
EPIDEMIOLOGY Rodolfo Saracci
ETHICS Simon Blackburn
EUGENICS Philippa Levine
THE EUROPEAN UNION John Pinder
    and Simon Usherwood
EVOLUTION Brian and
    Deborah Charlesworth
EXISTENTIALISM Thomas Flynn
FASCISM Kevin Passmore
FEMINISM Margaret Walters
THE FIRST WORLD WAR
    Michael Howard
FORENSIC PSYCHOLOGY
    David Canter
FOUCAULT Gary Gutting
FREE SPEECH Nigel Warburton
FREE WILL Thomas Pink
FREUD Anthony Storr
FUNDAMENTALISM Malise Ruthven
FUNGI Nicholas P. Money
GALAXIES John Gribbin
GALILEO Stillman Drake
GAME THEORY Ken Binmore
GANDHI Bhikhu Parekh
GEOGRAPHY John Matthews and
    David Herbert
GEOPOLITICS Klaus Dodds
GLOBAL CATASTROPHES Bill McGuire
GLOBAL ECONOMIC HISTORY
    Robert C. Allen
GLOBALIZATION Manfred Steger
GOD John Bowker
HABERMAS James Gordon Finlayson
HEGEL Peter Singer
HINDUISM Kim Knott
HISTORY John H. Arnold
THE HISTORY OF LIFE Michael Benton
THE HISTORY OF MATHEMATICS
    Jacqueline Stedall
THE HISTORY OF MEDICINE
    William Bynum
THE HISTORY OF TIME
    Leofranc Holford-Strevens
HIV AND AIDS Alan Whiteside
HOLLYWOOD Peter Decherney
HUMAN ANATOMY
    Leslie Klenerman
HUMAN EVOLUTION Bernard Wood
HUMAN RIGHTS Andrew Clapham
IDEOLOGY Michael Freeden
INDIAN PHILOSOPHY Sue Hamilton
INFINITY Ian Stewart
INFORMATION Luciano Floridi
INNOVATION Mark Dodgson and
    David Gann
INTELLIGENCE Ian J. Deary
INTERNATIONAL
    MIGRATION Khalid Koser
INTERNATIONAL RELATIONS
    Paul Wilkinson
ISLAM Malise Ruthven
ISLAMIC HISTORY Adam Silverstein
JESUS Richard Bauckham
JOURNALISM Ian Hargreaves

JUDAISM Norman Solomon
JUNG Anthony Stevens
KABBALAH Joseph Dan
KANT Roger Scruton
KNOWLEDGE Jennifer Nagel
THE KORAN Michael Cook
LATE ANTIQUITY Gillian Clark
LAW Raymond Wacks
THE LAWS OF THERMODYNAMICS
    Peter Atkins
LEADERSHIP Keith Grint
LEARNING Mark Haselgrove
LIGHT Ian Walmsley
LINGUISTICS Peter Matthews
LITERARY THEORY Jonathan Culler
LOCKE John Dunn
LOGIC Graham Priest
MACHIAVELLI Quentin Skinner
MARTIN LUTHER Scott H. Hendrix
MARTYRDOM Jolyon Mitchell
MARX Peter Singer
MATHEMATICS Timothy Gowers
THE MEANING OF LIFE Terry Eagleton
MEASUREMENT David Hand
MEDICAL ETHICS Tony Hope
MEDIEVAL BRITAIN John Gillingham
    and Ralph A. Griffiths
MEDIEVAL LITERATURE
    Elaine Treharne
MEDIEVAL PHILOSOPHY
    John Marenbon
MEMORY Jonathan K. Foster
METAPHYSICS Stephen Mumford
MICROSCOPY Terence Allen
MILITARY JUSTICE Eugene R. Fidell
MODERN ART David Cottington
MODERN CHINA Rana Mitter
MODERN IRELAND Senia Pašeta
MODERN ITALY Anna Cento Bull
MODERN JAPAN
    Christopher Goto-Jones
MODERNISM Christopher Butler
MOLECULAR BIOLOGY Aysha Divan
    and Janice A. Royds
MOLECULES Philip Ball
MOONS David A. Rothery
MUSIC Nicholas Cook
MYTH Robert A. Segal
NEOLIBERALISM Manfred Steger and
    Ravi Roy

NEWTON Robert Iliffe
NIETZSCHE Michael Tanner
NORTH AMERICAN INDIANS
    Theda Perdue and Michael D. Green
NORTHERN IRELAND
    Marc Mulholland
NOTHING Frank Close
NUCLEAR PHYSICS Frank Close
NUTRITION David A. Bender
THE PALESTINIAN-ISRAELI
    CONFLICT Martin Bunton
PANDEMICS Christian W. McMillen
PARTICLE PHYSICS Frank Close
THE PERIODIC TABLE Eric R. Scerri
PHILOSOPHY Edward Craig
PHILOSOPHY IN THE ISLAMIC
    WORLD Peter Adamson
PHILOSOPHY OF LAW
    Raymond Wacks
PHILOSOPHY OF SCIENCE
    Samir Okasha
PHOTOGRAPHY Steve Edwards
PHYSICAL CHEMISTRY Peter Atkins
PLANETS David A. Rothery
PLATO Julia Annas
POLITICAL PHILOSOPHY David Miller
POLITICS Kenneth Minogue
POPULISM Cas Mudde and
    Cristóbal Rovira Kaltwasser
POSTCOLONIALISM Robert Young
POSTMODERNISM Christopher Butler
POSTSTRUCTURALISM
    Catherine Belsey
PREHISTORY Chris Gosden
PRESOCRATIC PHILOSOPHY
    Catherine Osborne
PSYCHIATRY Tom Burns
PSYCHOLOGY Gillian Butler and
    Freda McManus
PSYCHOTHERAPY Tom Burns and
    Eva Burns-Lundgren
PUBLIC HEALTH Virginia Berridge
QUANTUM THEORY
    John Polkinghorne
RACISM Ali Rattansi
THE REFORMATION Peter Marshall
RELATIVITY Russell Stannard
THE RENAISSANCE Jerry Brotton
RENAISSANCE ART
    Geraldine A. Johnson

REVOLUTIONS Jack A. Goldstone
RHETORIC Richard Toye
RISK Baruch Fischhoff and John Kadvany
RITUAL Barry Stephenson
RIVERS Nick Middleton
ROBOTICS Alan Winfield
ROMAN BRITAIN Peter Salway
THE ROMAN EMPIRE
    Christopher Kelly
THE ROMAN REPUBLIC
    David M. Gwynn
RUSSIAN HISTORY Geoffrey Hosking
THE RUSSIAN REVOLUTION
    S. A. Smith
SCHIZOPHRENIA Chris Frith and
    Eve Johnstone
SCIENCE AND RELIGION
    Thomas Dixon
SEXUALITY Véronique Mottier
SHAKESPEARE'S COMEDIES
    Bart van Es
SIKHISM Eleanor Nesbitt
SLEEP Steven W. Lockley and
    Russell G. Foster
SOCIAL AND CULTURAL
    ANTHROPOLOGY
    John Monaghan and Peter Just
SOCIAL PSYCHOLOGY Richard J. Crisp
SOCIAL WORK Sally Holland and
    Jonathan Scourfield
SOCIALISM Michael Newman
SOCIOLOGY Steve Bruce

SOCRATES C. C. W. Taylor
SOUND Mike Goldsmith
THE SOVIET UNION Stephen Lovell
THE SPANISH CIVIL WAR
    Helen Graham
SPANISH LITERATURE Jo Labanyi
STATISTICS David J. Hand
STUART BRITAIN John Morrill
SYMMETRY Ian Stewart
TAXATION Stephen Smith
TELESCOPES Geoff Cottrell
TERRORISM Charles Townshend
THEOLOGY David F. Ford
TIBETAN BUDDHISM
    Matthew T. Kapstein
THE TROJAN WAR Eric H. Cline
THE TUDORS John Guy
THE UNITED NATIONS
    Jussi M. Hanhimäki
THE U.S. CONGRESS Donald A. Ritchie
THE U.S. SUPREME COURT
    Linda Greenhouse
THE VIKINGS Julian Richards
VIRUSES Dorothy H. Crawford
WAR AND TECHNOLOGY
    Alex Roland
WILLIAM SHAKESPEARE
    Stanley Wells
WITCHCRAFT Malcolm Gaskill
THE WORLD TRADE
    ORGANIZATION Amrita Narlikar
WORLD WAR II Gerhard L. Weinberg

Richard Bauckham

JESUS

A Very Short Introduction

OXFORD
UNIVERSITY PRESS

OXFORD

UNIVERSITY PRESS

Great Clarendon Street, Oxford OX2 6DP

Oxford University Press is a department of the University of Oxford.
It furthers the University's objective of excellence in research, scholarship,
and education by publishing worldwide in

Oxford New York

Auckland Cape Town Dar es Salaam Hong Kong Karachi
Kuala Lumpur Madrid Melbourne Mexico City Nairobi
New Delhi Shanghai Taipei Toronto

With offices in

Argentina Austria Brazil Chile Czech Republic France Greece
Guatemala Hungary Italy Japan Poland Portugal Singapore
South Korea Switzerland Thailand Turkey Ukraine Vietnam

Oxford is a registered trade mark of Oxford University Press
in the UK and in certain other countries

Published in the United States
by Oxford University Press Inc., New York

© Richard Bauckham 2011

The moral rights of the author have been asserted
Database right Oxford University Press (maker)

First published 2011

British Library Cataloguing in Publication Data

Data available

Library of Congress Cataloging in Publication Data

Data available

Typeset by SPI Publisher Services, Pondicherry, India
Printed in Great Britain
on acid-free paper by
Ashford Colour Press Ltd, Gosport, Hampshire

ISBN: 978–0–19–957527–5

10

Contents

Preface xi

List of illustrations xiii

1 Jesus – a universal icon 1

2 The sources 6

3 Jesus in his 1st-century context 18

4 Enacting the kingdom of God 35

5 Teaching the kingdom of God 57

6 A question of identity 84

7 Death and a new beginning 95

8 Jesus in Christian faith 110

Further reading 115

Index 121

Preface

Writing a book about Jesus is a daunting task. One could not begin to do justice to a figure who has for many centuries evoked the devotion of billions and in the last two centuries has been subjected to intense scholarly examination and debate. When I planned the book, I decided that its focus must be the historical Jesus of the Gospels, which is probably what most readers will expect, but that it is not the place to survey the many different approaches and results to be found in contemporary Jesus scholarship. I certainly do not want my readers to be unaware that there are many such, and that the approach I take in this book is as controversial as any of the others. But, rather than sketching many approaches inadequately, it seemed to me best to tell it as I see it. Essentially, this means reading the Gospels as versions of the history of Jesus (and by 'history', I mean the sort of history people wrote in the ancient world) in the context of all that we know of the 1st-century context in which Jesus actually lived. I take the Gospels to be based substantially on the testimony of the eyewitnesses who had known Jesus in his lifetime, and I briefly indicate the rationale for such an approach in Chapter 2, on sources. Rather than a minimal Jesus, reconstructed on the basis of a rather small selection of the data in the Gospels, as represented in many of the current scholarly accounts of the historical Jesus, I have tried to take seriously the different ways in which the four Gospels themselves portray Jesus. I take their differences to be an advantage: they give us more than one angle on a complex figure. I have not imagined that we can strip Jesus of all interpretation and get back to mere brute facts – or to more than a few facts that would be of little interest if they were all we knew – but I do think the Gospels give us access to the way Jesus was perceived by those who were close to him, people who experienced the events from the inside and whose own lives were deeply affected by them. This seems to me a kind of knowledge of Jesus that is well worth having, whatever we choose to do with it.

Richard Bauckham

List of illustrations

1 Jesus, 4th-century catacomb fresco **3**

2 Fragment of John's Gospel from c. AD 110 **11**
   © akg-images/www .BibleLandPictures.com

3 Inscription from Caesarea Maritima naming Pontius Pilate **19**
   © Almay/www.BibleLandPictures.com

4 A home in Nazareth from the time of Jesus **28**
   © Assaf Peretz, courtesy of Israel Antiquities Authority

5 Map of Palestine in the time of Jesus **32**

6 Jesus heals a haemorrhaging woman **39**
   Rome, Catacombs of Sts Marcellinus and Peter. Photo © 2010 Scala, Florence

7 A 1st-century fishing boat from the Sea of Galilee **48**
   © ANSA under licence from Archivi Fratelli Alinari

8 Model of 1st-century Jerusalem, with the Temple **80**

9 Jesus as the Good Shepherd **92**
   © akg-images/Erich Lessing

10 'Alexamenos worships his God' (graffito from Rome, c. AD 200) **96**
   Rome, Antiquarium of the Palatine. Photo © 2010 Scala, Florence, courtesy of the Ministero Beni e Att. Culturali

11 Ancient olive grove in Gethsemane **103**
   © Zev Radovan/www .BibleLandPictures.com

12 Ancient Jewish tomb **105**
   © Todd Bolen/www.BiblePlaces.com

Chapter 1
Jesus – a universal icon

Jesus of Nazareth, or Jesus Christ (as Christians call him), is
undoubtedly the best known and most influential human person
in world history. Two billion people today identify themselves as
Christians, with the implication that Jesus is the focus of their
relationship to God and of their way of living in the world. Such
followers of Jesus are now more numerous and make up a greater
proportion of the world's population than ever before. It is
estimated that they are increasing by some 70,000 persons every
day. This growth of Christianity is taking place despite its decline
in the West, especially in Western Europe, and those who think
the figure of Jesus Christ is of fading significance need to reckon
with the astonishingly rapid increase in numbers of Christian
believers in other parts of the world, such as Africa and (who
would have expected it?) China. Jesus is plainly no longer an icon
purely of Western culture, but in fact he never was. He lived in the
Middle East, and in the first few centuries of Christianity the faith
spread in all directions – not only to Greece and Rome, France
and Spain, but also to Egypt, North Africa, and Ethiopia, to
Turkey and Armenia, to Iraq, Persia, and India. Christianity was a
world religion long before it was a European one.

Thus Jesus has never been confined to Western religion and culture.
In fact, no other figure has so extensively crossed the cultural

divisions of humanity and found a place in so many diverse cultural contexts. When Jesus has been used to legitimate domination and oppression, very often the oppressed, like the black slaves of the American South, have been energized to resist by the solidarity of Jesus with them. While in the modern period Christianity has been all too easily identified with Western imperialism and colonialism, or with the spread of Western culture, the figure of Jesus himself has had a way of escaping these associations. The search for an African Jesus, an Indian Jesus, a Japanese Jesus goes on, while people inspired by Jesus continue to find him in the poor, the sick, and the dying, wherever and whoever they are.

Jesus is not even confined to Christianity. He is a figure of significance in Islam, a messenger of God who appears in the Qur'an. Many Hindus and Buddhists have interpreted him favourably within the perspectives of their own traditions. Recently, some Jewish thinkers have been reclaiming Jesus as an authentically Jewish teacher. There have been appreciative Marxist readings of Jesus. There are New Age versions of Jesus. Moreover, respecting Jesus while denouncing the church has become a common attitude in the secular West. He is usually exempted from the charge that religion is a bad influence, promoting bigotry and violence. It is still advantageous to claim Jesus as support for one's cause, though more so in the United States than in Britain or northern Europe.

No other individual has inspired so much art, literature, music, and even film. There are the wonderfully varied traditions of visual portrayal of Jesus in Byzantine and Russian icons, in Ethiopian church art, in the sculpture and stained glass of the medieval West, in Renaissance painting, in the Christian art of Africa, Latin America, and India. But such has been the impact of the figure of Jesus that it has gone far beyond exclusive or explicit portrayal of Jesus the Lord or Saviour. In art, he may stand for universal humanity; his passion and death may convey the message that Calvary is everywhere; the peculiar horrors of

1. **Jesus, depicted in a 4th-century catacomb fresco**

modern history may find expression in a crucifix. In literature, there are innumerable Christ figures, with sufficient family resemblance to be readily recognizable as such. Such art and literature may be unconnected with religious faith but still bear the imprint of the doctrine of the incarnation, that is, of the Christ who identifies with all humanity, sharing the common humanity and the common plight of all people. Despite the profound forgetfulness of Jesus in the popular culture of contemporary Europe, people still connect with his story when it is told. Jesus films are invariably controversial, but can be very successful nonetheless, as can Jesus musicals.

Even a small sampling of this historical and contemporary wealth of images of Jesus reveals their stunning variety. Has Jesus in the end become no more than an empty vessel that can be filled with any sort of content? It is not surprising that among all the images there are some very strange ones that have little resemblance to others. In the 1960s, Dead Sea Scrolls scholar John Allegro proposed that Jesus was actually a hallucinogenic mushroom! Such curiosities from the lunatic fringe of Jesus speculation come and go and are forgotten. But what, for example, of the many African portrayals of a black Christ? To understand these, one should realize that there is no intention of suggesting that Jesus the Jew who lived in Palestine in the 1st century was actually a black African. What is being expressed is the connection, perceived in African Christian faith, between Jesus the universal Saviour and black people. What is being portrayed is the loving solidarity of Christ who identifies in love with all people, black people included.

This example suggests at least part of the explanation of the variety of images of Jesus in the different periods and cultural contexts of Christianity. These images express the relevance that the figure of Jesus was felt to have in different contexts. The exceptionally tortured and bloody portrayals of the suffering Christ in the late medieval period belong to a society ravaged by plague and war. Believers found in Christ a God who came to be with them in their pain. But such an emphasis would not have been possible had the Gospels not portrayed Jesus as having suffered and died in excruciating pain. At least within the mainstream Christian traditions, such images of Christ were always inspired and resourced by the Gospels. They portray not just figure anyone could imagine or desire, but the Christ of the Gospels as he seemed most closely to connect with believers in that time and place.

From the perspective of Christian faith, such a procedure has its dangers. What to make, for example, of the Aryan Christ of the

German Christians of the Nazi period? Some images of Jesus so distort the Christ of the Gospels as to be unrecognizable as him. They are an ideological abuse of Jesus, putting him to uses wholly inconsistent with the figure to be found in the Gospels. So the Gospels have always been, not only a resource, but also a means of critique of images of Jesus. And since the images can never portray more than one aspect of the depth and complexity of the Jesus of the Gospels, Christians have gone back to them constantly in order to fund their imagination of Jesus from the wealth of stories and sayings to be found there.

In the end, it is the four Gospels in the New Testament that have inspired, directly or indirectly, virtually every image of Jesus both within the church and outside. It makes sense for our strategy in this book to go back to the Gospels and to draw from them our picture of Jesus as he was in history. But here we also encounter another phenomenon: the 'quest of the historical Jesus' in scholarly research over the last two centuries. Many scholars have sought the Jesus of history not in the Gospels as such but by excavating the history behind the Gospels and reconstructing a picture of the real Jesus from what they regard as the more historically reliable material in the Gospels. We shall take up this issue in the next chapter.

Chapter 2
The sources

The account of Jesus in this book will be based on the view that the four Gospels in our New Testament are substantially reliable sources for knowing quite a lot about Jesus. This is a controversial view that is contested by many scholars. In this chapter, I shall sketch my reasons for taking it. But it is worth saying at the start that to some extent the proof of this pudding is in the eating. Readers may not be equipped to adjudicate for themselves the detailed historical arguments that go into the making of any account of Jesus, but they can tell whether the result is a coherent and convincing portrait of a remarkable historical figure.

They can also appreciate that history is never a mere collection of facts but an exercise in interpretation. Our earliest and best sources for knowing about Jesus are already interpretations; there is no way they could not be. Even the people who knew and first talked about him to others were interpreting him; they could not have talked about him otherwise. But this does not mean there is no difference between good history and bad history, or that one interpretation is as good as another. We all know there is a difference between newspaper reports that are based on careful and accurate investigation and those that, for reasons of carelessness or bias or the pursuit of sensationalism, grossly distort the facts. In the first case, we know that the reporter is telling us how she sees it, but we trust that she is honestly and intelligently and with well-honed skills providing an account that does justice to the evidence.

The four Gospels and the other Gospels

Many people in contemporary Western society have recently gained the impression that the four Gospels in the New Testament are rather unreliable sources for knowing much about Jesus and that there are other sources that give a very different and more trustworthy picture. Dan Brown's amazingly successful novel *The Da Vinci Code* popularized this view, though he certainly didn't invent it. Many people who may never have read any of the Gospels now think the so-called 'Gnostic Gospels' contain the real truth about Jesus.

The Gnostic Gospels became known after their discovery at Nag Hammadi in Egypt in 1945–6. It will be a useful introduction to both bodies of literature to compare and contrast, on the one hand, the New Testament Gospels of Matthew, Mark, Luke, and John, and, on the other hand, the Gnostic Gospels attributed to Mary, Thomas, Judas, and others. (Besides these Gospels that can be rather loosely called Gnostic, there were other Gospels more like the New Testament Gospels, but only fragments of them have survived.)

First, what sort of books are they? In terms of literary genre, the four New Testament Gospels and the Gnostic Gospels are very different kinds of work. The four Gospels all tell a continuous narrative about the historical person Jesus, beginning either with the outset of his public career or with his birth, continuing until his death on a Roman cross, and ending with accounts either of the discovery that his tomb was empty or of his appearances after death. Within such an overall narrative framework, stories of Jesus' activity and his teachings (whether in public or to his disciples) are collected. This is the kind of work that early readers or hearers would have identified as a biography–the life of a famous person (though ancient biographies did not have all the characteristics we associate with modern biographies).

The Gnostic Gospels are very different. There is very little narrative, and no attempt to tell the story of Jesus' historical life. Most are set after the resurrection of Jesus, and portray the risen Christ teaching his disciples (or a few or one of them) in long discourses or dialogues. We could call them 'revelation discourses'. Most of these works tell or imply the Gnostic myth of redemption, according to which this material world was made by an ill-intentioned demigod who bungled the job. Jesus was a supernatural emissary from the unknown high God, the Father, who came to enlighten those human beings, the Gnostics, who are trapped in this material world but truly belong with the Father in his transcendent world. Jesus brings them the knowledge of their true identity. The Gnostic Christ was not really human, but merely adopted human forms in order to appear in this world. He did not, for example, die. So verbal revelation, not human history, is what interested the Gnostics. Whereas the four Gospels provide a richly detailed portrait of a real human life in a specific time and place, the Gnostic Gospels abstract the figure of Jesus into an almost purely mythical world.

Secondly, however, the Gnostic Gospels do presuppose that the story and sayings of Jesus before his resurrection were well known. Their attitude to the well-known teaching of Jesus is that it was inferior teaching for the general public or that its real, esoteric meaning was not made known at the time. The Gnostic Gospels report Jesus' real message, his esoteric teaching to the disciples, which had then been transmitted secretly to the Gnostic teachers of the 2nd century. In order to find a place for this additional, secret teaching in the well-known story of Jesus, the Gnostic Gospels take advantage of the fact that, according to that story, Jesus did teach his disciples after the resurrection. The New Testament Gospels, however, report little of what he said. This was an obvious opportunity for later writers who wished to attribute more teaching to Jesus, especially if it was to be depicted as special, esoteric teaching for the disciples alone. The Gnostic Gospels, therefore, were designed to *add*. They are subsequent to the four Gospels not only chronologically but also logically.

Thirdly, another striking contrast between the two sorts of Gospel is that the four Gospels connect the story of Jesus closely with the story of Israel in the Hebrew Bible. The God whom Jesus calls Father is the God of Israel, and Jesus identifies strongly with the people of Israel. The four Gospels depict him as the Messiah of Israel who is also the Messiah for the non-Jewish nations. The Gnostic Gospels sharply disconnect Jesus from the story of Israel, for a very good reason. For them, the Old Testament God is the inferior creator of this material world, from whose power the Gnostic is to be delivered by the enlightenment Jesus brings from the true supreme God, a God not known to the Hebrew Bible. Inevitably, the Jewishness of Jesus, which is integral to his portrayal in the four Gospels, disappears from the Gnostic Gospels.

Finally, a key consequence of these differences is that the Gnostic Gospels scarcely attempt to set Jesus in a real historical context (their few attempts to do so are clearly derivative and sometimes erroneous), whereas the four Gospels embed their narrative of Jesus in an historical context that can be verified. The Jesus of these Gospels belongs to the Palestinian Jewish world of the early 1st century AD, with its religious customs and rules, its factions and beliefs, its religious and political leaders, its uneasy subjection to Roman authority, even its farming practices. The four Gospels present a Jesus who is thoroughly credible within his time and place. They have every appearance of being good history. The Gnostic Gospels do not.

There is just one of the Gospels found at Nag Hammadi, the Gospel of Thomas, that has more of a claim to be taken seriously as an historical source for Jesus, and some scholars do take it seriously. Though it has scarcely more historical context than the others, it consists of a collection of sayings of Jesus, many of which resemble those in the four Gospels. In my view, it is best explained as a selection of sayings of Jesus that could be interpreted in a Gnostic way. It may transmit some of these sayings independently of the four Gospels, but its value is very uncertain.

Are the four Gospels good sources?

The key question for assessing the historical value of the New Testament Gospels is: how did these traditions about Jesus, the stories and sayings, reach the authors of the Gospels? Jesus probably died in AD 30 (though some scholars argue for AD 27 or 33), and what is probably the earliest of the four Gospels, Mark's, is usually thought to have been written around AD 65–75. Matthew's and Luke's Gospels date from at least a little later in the 1st century, while John's Gospel, almost certainly the last of the four to be written (or at least completed), is probably to be dated in the last decade of the century. A large majority of scholars think that Matthew and Luke used Mark as a major source of their own work, though they drew extensively on other sources as well.

So a few decades separate the events of Jesus' career from the Gospels. What happened to the traditions about him during that period? For a century, Gospels scholarship has been dominated by a particular answer to that question that was given by a few eminent scholars, called the form critics, early in the 20th century. In my view, the form critics set mainstream Gospels scholarship on a false track, but only quite recently have a number of scholars seriously undertaken to correct the form critics' mistakes.

Absolutely fundamental for the form critics' approach was their conviction that the Gospels are folk literature, derived from oral traditions, which they compared with the material studied by the

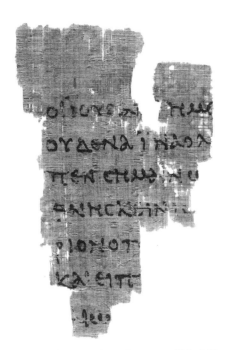

2. The earliest Gospel manuscript, a fragment of John's Gospel from c. AD 110

folklorists of their day. Oral tradition, they thought, was formed and transmitted by the folk, not by individuals, and the communities that valued such folklore had no interest of any kind in history. By analogy, the Jesus traditions were anonymous community traditions, passed down in the early Christian communities, not connected to individuals such as those who had been eyewitnesses of Jesus' history, but only to the local Christian community itself. They were transmitted not by people concerned to relate past history, but for purposes orientated solely to the communities' present, and could therefore be freely modified or even created *de novo* in accordance with the communities' present needs.

This view of the way that traditions about Jesus reached the writers of the Gospels has made it very difficult to use the Gospels as historical sources for knowing about the 'real' historical Jesus. While some scholars have argued that the oral transmission of traditions preserved them rather faithfully, others have thought that much of the material in the Gospels must be attributed to the early church, rather than to Jesus. In any case, it could certainly not be taken for granted that the Jesus of the Gospels – or the Jesuses of the four Gospels – really corresponds with the so-called historical Jesus, the Jesus who actually lived in 1st-century Jewish Palestine. Reconstructing this historical Jesus became a difficult task, requiring each story and each saying in the Gospels to be individually assessed for its authenticity. Scholars have devised and debated various criteria for distinguishing authentic and inauthentic material in the Gospels.

The results have been very disappointing because scholars pursuing this enterprise have come up with, not one, but many different 'historical Jesuses'. One book about the historical Jesus recently listed some of the options:

> ...an eschatological prophet, a Galilean holy man, an occultic magician, an innovative rabbi, a trance-inducing psychotherapist, a Jewish sage, a political revolutionary, an Essene conspirator, an itinerant exorcist, an historicized myth, a protoliberation theologian, a peasant artisan, a Torah-observant Pharisee, a Cynic-like philosopher, a self-conscious eschatological agent, a socioeconomic reformer, a paradoxical Messianic claimant and...one who saw himself as...the very embodiment of Yahweh-God.
>
> James K. Beilby and Paul Rhodes Eddy (eds.), *The Historical Jesus: Five Views* (London: SPCK, 2010), p. 53

Admittedly some of these are much more plausible than others, and they are not all mutually exclusive, but the fact that such diverse results have come out of the 'quest of the historical Jesus' conducted on form-critical premises does not inspire confidence in the historical methods being used.

The major problem is that each story and each saying has to be individually assessed for its authenticity, but we simply do not have the means to adequately do this in most cases. Each scholar makes their own selection of authentic material and constructs an historical Jesus on that basis. The selections often seem fairly arbitrary or else trapped in a vicious circle in which the sort of figure a scholar is inclined to think Jesus was strongly influences that scholar's selection of authentic material. The result is often a very 'thin' portrayal of Jesus, as opposed to the richly complex portrayals that the Gospels themselves provide.

Is there a way beyond this impasse? Fortunately, some of the key ideas of the form critics have been much criticized in recent scholarship, and we need no longer take them for granted. For example, they used a model of oral tradition that was based on cases like the transmission of European folktales (over many centuries and anonymously). We now know much more about oral tradition, from many societies across the world, and what the form critics thought had to be true may not be the case at all. Oral tradition takes many forms and it is hard to generalize. Moreover, since the Gospels were written within the lifetime of people who had witnessed the events, they are better characterized as oral history. That links them with the way good historians in the ancient world worked, by interviewing eyewitnesses and incorporating the testimony of eyewitnesses into their work.

In my view, the key to a viable alternative to form criticism is to be found in the eyewitnesses. All scholars agree that Gospel traditions must originally have been formulated by disciples of Jesus and others who encountered him, witnessed the events, and remembered his teaching. But for the form critics, the eyewitnesses immediately drop out of the picture and the anonymous collectives of the early churches take control of the oral tradition, developing it more or less at will for the needs of the community. This picture is very implausible, because the eyewitnesses were certainly still alive and well long after the traditions originated, and many of them were very well known in the early Christian movement. They would have remained the authoritative sources and guardians of the Jesus traditions, a role that is common in oral societies, and they are the people from whom the writers of the Gospels are likely to have derived their material.

There is no need to suppose that the traditions passed through innumerable hands before reaching the Gospel writers. The latter may well have received many traditions from eyewitnesses themselves, or at least through only one intermediary, oral or written. In fact, this is what the preface to Luke's Gospel suggests, claiming to record the events 'just as they have been delivered to us by those who from the beginning were eyewitnesses'. The probable dates of the Gospels (along with the probability that the authors would have been collecting the traditions long before they completed the writing of their Gospels) make it entirely plausible that the texts of the Gospels as we have them are at no great distance from the reports of the eyewitnesses. These probable dates of the Gospels also make it likely that they were written precisely because the eyewitnesses were dying and their authoritative testimony needed to be preserved in writing. In my view, one of the Gospel writers, John, was himself an eyewitness and completed his Gospel near the end of his life as the fruit of a lifetime of reflecting on his memories of Jesus.

Such a model of the way the Gospels were based on eyewitness sources opens the door to a fresh reading of the Gospels that can bring to light the ways in which they themselves often indicate their eyewitness sources. The naming of the person from whom a particular story derived is one such method. But this model also enables us to treat the early church's traditions about the origins and authorship of the Gospels more seriously. Before form criticism, scholars did take such traditions seriously, but they were dismissed by the form critics because they did not fit the form critics' model of how the Gospels came to be. The earliest such testimony is in the fragments (sadly all that we now have) of the work of Papias, bishop of Hierapolis at the beginning of the 2nd century. He reported that Mark was Peter's interpreter (who presumably translated Peter's Aramaic into Greek or Latin) and based his Gospel on Peter's accounts of the activity and teaching of Jesus. I have argued that this claim is confirmed by the Gospel of Mark itself when we look carefully at the place and role of Peter within this Gospel. If Mark's Gospel was closely associated with Peter, this would account for the high value that Matthew and Luke evidently placed on it, adopting most of its content into their own Gospels.

Elsewhere I have presented a full case for treating the Gospels as substantially the testimony of the eyewitnesses. One further, important comment that needs to be made here is that the word *testimony* is important. The eyewitnesses from whom these Gospels derive were not disinterested observers. They were involved participants in the events they later recalled and narrated. They were committed believers in the Jesus whose story they told. They and the Gospel writers were thoughtful interpreters of the significance of that story for human salvation. Moreover, they told the story of Jesus in order to evoke or to inform faith in Jesus. These facts do not disqualify the Gospels from being considered history. I have already mentioned that the best way of categorizing the Gospels as literature is to see them as biographies, more precisely biographies of a contemporary person, based (as such biographies were expected to be) on eyewitness testimony. Such biographies were usually written in order to edify or to inspire. The subject may, for example, be held up as a moral example that others should imitate. The life of a philosopher may be intended to recommend his philosophy. While the kind of message the Gospels were written to convey may be unusual, the fact that they do have a message was not. The history is interpreted, of course, but it is *history* that it is interpreted. Moreover, the testimony of the eyewitnesses was precisely the kind of testimony that was valued by ancient historians – that of involved participants, people who could convey something of the reality of the events from the inside.

The category of testimony is probably the most useful way to think of the kind of material we read in the Gospels. The material comes from people who witnessed the events and were deeply affected by them. Fact and meaning were inseparable in their memory and telling of their stories. For them, these were life-changing events that they felt impelled to communicate. More especially, of course, it was Jesus who had made on them the overwhelming impact they sought to convey when they remembered his teaching and recounted their stories about him.

None of this means that we should accept uncritically whatever the Gospels tell us about Jesus. It does mean that the practice of Jesus scholars who have tried to weigh the authenticity of each saying and story individually was mistaken. But that is not how historians generally assess evidence. What historians look for are reasons for trusting or distrusting any particular source. It is never possible to verify every part of what, for example, is reported by someone who claims to have lived through a series of events. What we can do is to assess whether that person's testimony is generally trustworthy. This is the approach we should take with the Gospels. If we are satisfied, for example, that Mark's Gospel derives from a good source (Peter's account of the events he experienced), then we must ask: do Peter (as the major source) and Mark (as the author who has preserved Peter's testimony) appear to be generally trustworthy?

One way of answering that question is to use our knowledge of early 1st-century Jewish Palestine to assess whether the Gospels fit that context. Owing to archaeology, the Dead Sea Scrolls, and other Jewish literature of the period, our knowledge of that context has improved considerably in recent decades. Do the Gospels reflect the society in which their stories are set? Are their detailed references to aspects of that society accurate? Does Jesus as they portray him credibly belong in that context? Such questions are all the more apt because we know that Jewish Palestine changed very considerably after the Jewish revolt against Rome that began in AD 66 and led to the destruction of Jerusalem and its Temple in AD 70. Good eyewitness testimony should preserve memories of how things were in Galilee and Judaea in the time of Jesus. In my judgement, the Gospels – all four of them – pass this test very well, though much detailed work still remains to be done on this question. In the next chapter, as a preliminary to our study of Jesus, we shall sketch the 1st-century context in which the historical Jesus lived. This will give some indication of how the Gospel accounts of Jesus fit that context.

In the chapters that follow, I draw freely on all the Gospels for my account of Jesus. However, I have not ignored the fact that, as all careful readers of the Gospels soon discover, John's is a rather different sort of Gospel from the other three. (The relative similarity of these three is why they are known collectively as the Synoptic Gospels.) I rate highly John's narrative of events, partly because of the accuracy and precision in chronological and geographical matters that distinguish John from the Synoptics. I do not think John invents events for theological purposes. However, I do think John is a more interpretative Gospel than the others, and none the worse for that. So when it comes to the discourses of Jesus in John, I have been more cautious. Whereas the Synoptics usually preserve the sayings of Jesus as his disciples learned and remembered them, varying and expanding them for interpretative purposes only to a quite limited degree, John seems to avail himself of the permission generally allowed ancient historians to put into his own words the sort of thing Jesus would have said. So the discourses of Jesus in John are peppered with traditional sayings on which John has expanded with his own reflective interpretation. The more interpretative nature of John's Gospel makes it appropriate, on occasion, to treat this Gospel's handling of a topic separately from that of the Synoptics.

Chapter 3
Jesus in his 1st-century context

We are fortunate in knowing a lot about the context in Jewish Palestine in the 1st century AD in which Jesus lived. The interpretation of some of the evidence is debatable, but in general we can build up a rather accurate picture of the world in which the Gospels set their accounts of Jesus. That these accounts fit that picture in the many detailed references they themselves make to features of Jesus' religious, political, and cultural context is one good reason for rating highly their historical reliability.

Political and religious context

Jewish Palestine came under the expanding rule of the Roman Empire in 63 BC, when the Roman general Pompey conquered Jerusalem and made a bad start to Rome's dealings with the Jews in their land by violating the sanctity of the Temple. During Jesus' adult life, Judaea, the heartland of Jewish territory around Jerusalem, was under the direct rule of a Roman governor (Pontius Pilate at the time of Jesus' public activity), while the rest of Palestine was entrusted to puppet rulers loyal to Rome,

3. Inscription from Caesarea Maritima naming Pontius Pilate

members of the Herodian family. Galilee was ruled by Herod Antipas, whom Jesus once called 'that fox'.

That Rome ruled her empire with relative tolerance for local customs and cultures did not prevent many Jews in Palestine from objecting, on religio-political principle, to the subjection of God's people to pagan rulers, especially rulers who claimed divinity and an empire that attributed its success to pagan gods. Roman rule impacted ordinary people most in the form of taxation, which would have been regarded not as a contribution to the public good, but as a burden on peasant farmers living close to subsistence. As a later Jewish commentator put it, 'the Romans built fine bridges in order to collect the tolls'. The benefits of peace and prosperity that Rome claimed to give its subjects could not obscure the fact that the empire served primarily the prosperity of the Romans and the local elites who supported them.

Rome usually governed the provinces in collaboration with the local elites. So it was natural that in Judaea the Romans enlisted the support of the high priest and his council, which was made up of the leading aristocrats, mostly members of the chief priestly caste, but also included heads of wealthy lay families (Joseph of Arimathea and Nicodemus are examples in the Gospels).

Common Judaism

Although there was a good deal of variety in the faith and practice of Jews, the most important elements were shared by most. There must have been a strong sense of belonging to one people with a special religious calling, especially as a result of worship in the Temple in Jerusalem. In the rituals and especially the annual festivals in the Temple, Jews of almost every description participated together and were conscious of a common identity. This was true even for the large number of Jews who lived in the diaspora communities scattered across most of the known world. Many went on pilgrimage to the Temple, while many others sent their Temple tax, which helped to finance the sacrifices. As for Jews in Palestine, it was probably not possible for people such as peasant farmers to attend three annual festivals in the Temple, as the law of Moses required of adult males. But most would make pilgrimage to the Temple when they could, and the experience of one of the festivals must often have been the most exciting experience they had in that year.

The Temple was the symbolic centre of Jewish faith and it was also the place where God was accessible to his people in a special way. It was God's holy presence in the Temple that made Jerusalem the holy city and Palestine the holy land. It was God's presence in the Temple that made it the only place where sacrifice could be offered. The festivals were partly agricultural, but also they commemorated the key events of Israel's origins. Passover, for example, commemorated the Exodus, when Moses had led the people of Israel out of slavery in Egypt. The festivals would help to instil in people a strong sense of being part of a national story, which was also told in the Hebrew Scriptures. Especially, they would know how God called Abraham, freed Abraham's descendants from Egyptian oppression, gave them the covenant at Mount Sinai that made them his people, and gave them also the land of Israel. This story would have a strong contemporary relevance for Jews conscious of Roman oppression, and many hoped for a new Exodus, when God would free them once again from the pagan yoke and give them back the land that Rome had taken over. Evidently what some people expected of Jesus was a new Exodus of this kind. It is noteworthy that it was in the context of the huge numbers of pilgrims thronging Jerusalem for the Passover festival that the authorities decided Jesus was too dangerous a figure to be left alive. Passover was a time not only to remember God's liberation of Israel from Egypt but also to hope for his liberation of his people from Rome.

Among the defining features of the common Judaism that a very large majority of Jews shared were monotheism and the Torah. In a world where religious cults were usually seen as quite compatible with each other, Jews were an oddity. They stubbornly maintained that their God was the only God and that his cult was incompatible with any others, since all other objects of worship were false gods. Devout Jews recited every day the biblical passage known as the *Shema*: 'Hear, O Israel, YHWH our God, YHWH is one. You shall love YHWH your God with all your heart, and with all your soul, and with all your might' (Deuteronomy 6:4–5). This must have kept Jews highly conscious both of the uniqueness of their God and also of the demand for total and exclusive devotion that he made on his people. Jesus singled out this very passage as the most important of all God's commandments. (By this period, Jews considered the divine name too holy to pronounce, and, since only its four consonants were written, it is best to represent it as YHWH.)

Although he was the God of Israel, this God was no petty tribal deity. He was the Creator of all things and the supreme Sovereign over all things. He had purposes not only for Israel but for all the nations. But he had chosen the people of Israel as his 'special possession', and had given them the law of Moses, the Torah (the first five books of the Bible), which enabled them to live as God's distinctively holy people (where 'holy' means 'dedicated to YHWH'). The 613 commandments of the Torah cover the whole scope of human life, individual and social. They range from detailed cultic commandments for sacrifice and worship to dietary rules, criminal law, and stringent moral requirements. The Ten Commandments were often seen as the quintessence of the law. In theory, the Torah was to regulate the whole of Jewish life.

Jewish expectations of the future, based on the prophecies in the Hebrew Bible, included the hope that all the nations would one day acknowledge the God of Israel as the true and only God. In the situation of the 1st century AD , it is not surprising that hopes for the future focused on the downfall of the nations that oppressed Israel, though this did not necessarily include all nations. The conversion of the nations was sometimes envisaged as a kind of enslavement under a Jewish empire. But there was also much in the Hebrew Bible to nourish a generous expectation that, through the witness of Israel's loyalty to the true God, the nations would turn to him and also become his peoples. We should also note that one did not have to be a Jew by birth to belong to God's holy people. Gentiles could convert, and many did so. Narrow nationalism was not intrinsic to ancient Judaism, even though was one current in the diversity of Jewish attitudes at this time.

Finally, something should be said about ritual (or cultic) purity, a topic that is sometimes explicit and often implicit in the Gospel accounts of Jesus' teaching. Impurity is best thought of as a sort of invisible dirt that people picked up through contact with various things. Odd as it seems to us, many traditional peoples have ideas about ritual purity. In the Jewish version, one contracted impurity through contact with corpses, sexual fluids, other genital discharges, skin disease, and, in the case of women, through childbirth. This does not make such things sinful; in most cases, it was not wrong to contract impurity. Often it was unavoidable. Having sex, bearing children, and burying the dead were seen not only as good things, but as positive duties. The only consequence of contracting impurity was that one had to remove it, usually through immersion in water.

Originally, purity and impurity only really mattered when one visited the Temple. God's presence in the Temple made it a kind of pure space that would be defiled by someone in a state of impurity. But by the 1st century AD, there was a tendency to think that, since purity was a good thing, one should aim at being pure as much as possible. All over Palestine, archaeologists have found ritual baths, which indicate that it was not just groups such as the Pharisees who cared about purity. Many ordinary people evidently took care to remove impurity when they contracted it. It was part of the desire to be the holy people of the holy God.

The Jewish parties

Most Jews did not identify with any specific version of Judaism, but there were groups that held to particular interpretations of Jewish religion. Since Torah was a defining feature of Jewish identity, and all Jews sought to live by it, the differences between the groups often focused on issues of interpretation of Torah. Interpretation of Torah was essential if it was to be practised. God forbade Israel to work on the Sabbath, but what exactly counted as work in this context? Such questions gave scope for endless debate, which can sound esoteric but was intended to settle what should be done in practice.

The Jewish historian Josephus identified and described four main parties within Palestinian Judaism: Pharisees, Sadducees, Essenes, and a fourth category to which he gives no name. Since of all the parties the Pharisees were the most influential, and since they are also the group that feature most prominently in the Gospels, they will receive the most attention here.

The Pharisees had a reputation for being the most exact or precise interpreters of the law (though this does not mean they always gave it the most rigorous interpretation). They were specialists in defining precisely what the law required in daily life. They also treated as binding a body of oral traditions handed down from Pharisaic teachers of the past. Evidently they were influential. Many people who were not Pharisees respected them and followed their interpretation of Torah to some extent. They were not, like the Essenes, who also interpreted the law very precisely, a separatist sect content to cultivate their own holiness in isolation. The Pharisees seem to have been more like a movement with a programme of holiness for the nation. In the time of Jesus, they had no institutional power base from which to impose their interpretation of Judaism, but they were teachers widely respected for their own consistent practice of their interpretations of Torah.

The key question for Jews during this period was: how were they to be the holy people of God in the situation of Roman occupation? The Pharisees seem to have given prominence to ritual purity, and especially to eating meals in a state of purity. They greatly extended the purity rules in the Torah and made purity a major concern of daily life. Purity was no longer just a matter for the priests and for ordinary people when they visited the Temple. The Pharisees aimed at the greatest degree of purity that was possible in ordinary life for people who were not priests. Purity was by no means their only concern. They also defined what was required to be a holy people in such matters as the tithing of agricultural produce, observance of the Sabbath, and Temple practice. All these were Jewish distinctives that would mark out God's people as different from the Gentiles who defiled the holy land by practising idolatry and other abominations.

In a situation of political powerlessness, the Pharisaic programme could have been seen as the most effective way to resist the Roman occupation. It promoted increased holiness in those areas of life over which people did have control, such as meals, agriculture, and family life. The Pharisees did not renounce the expectation that sooner or later God must deliver his people from pagan rule and restore their theocratic independence. Perhaps their programme of national renewal was intended to make the Jews fit for such divine intervention. Some Pharisees are known to have become involved in military rebellion against Rome, but how far Pharisees in general favoured such an approach is unknown.

The Essenes, however, certainly did. At least, that is the case if the Dead Sea Scrolls are, as most scholars think, the library of a monastic-style community of Essenes on the shores of the Dead Sea. This group was preparing to fight a holy war, with divine assistance, against the Romans, and lived by an extremely rigorous interpretation of Torah. The majority of Essenes lived in the towns and villages of Jewish Palestine, but still formed exclusive communities that kept apart from their non-Essene neighbours. This must be the reason why no Essenes feature in any of the accounts of the career of Jesus. Unlike the Pharisees, they were not in the synagogues and market places where Jewish teachers encountered and debated with each other.

The Sadducees do make an appearance in the Gospels, debating with Jesus a point that distinguished them from most other Jews in this period. They did not believe in life beyond death, and this seems to have been a consequence of their 'fundamentalist' view of Scripture. They professed to believe only what was taught in the five books of Moses and to practise only the letter of the law of Moses. They were probably no more than a few hundred members of wealthy aristocratic families.

It is commonly thought that the high priest and other high-ranking Temple officials in this period were usually Sadducees, and so, if this is correct, the Sadducees dominated the Jewish government of Judaea under the superior authority of the Roman governor. Sadducees had political power but their religious views were not influential.

Finally, the Jewish party that Josephus fails to name are the political revolutionaries. (They have often been called 'the Zealots', but this seems to be a misuse of the term.) According to Josephus, they arose at the time (AD 6) when direct Roman rule over Judaea was introduced and a tax assessment undertaken in preparation for levying the Roman tribute. A movement led by Judas the Galilean held that revolt against Rome was a religious duty stemming from the first of the Ten Commandments ('You shall have no other gods beside me'). To pay taxes to Rome was to acknowledge Rome's claim to own the holy land of Israel that actually belongs only to God. Judas' revolt was suppressed, but its ideology forms the potent background to the occasion when enemies of Jesus asked him whether it was right to pay taxes to Caesar.

Josephus was writing in the aftermath of the Jewish revolt against Rome that led to the destruction of Jerusalem and the Temple in AD 70. He had a strong interest in showing that Judaism as such did not entail opposition to Rome and the revolt did not have roots in the teaching of major Jewish groups. He therefore put the blame on a minority, Judas the Galilean and his successors, whose ideas were not widely shared. It seems likely that sympathy for armed revolt against Rome was more widespread – certainly among Essenes, perhaps among Pharisees, and surely among the common people. But we should also remember that it was quite possible for Jews to hope for the removal of the Roman yoke not by revolutionary activity but by miraculous divine intervention, comparable with what had happened at the Exodus from Egypt. Though Galilee and Judaea may have been relatively peaceful during the time of Jesus' adult life, we should not underestimate the simmering resentment of Roman rule, of which both the Roman and the Jewish authorities would have been well aware.

Galilee

Jesus grew up in an insignificant Jewish village in Galilee, called Nazareth. It was home to fewer than four hundred people, almost all farmers. A house from the time of Jesus was excavated recently. With two rooms and a courtyard where a cistern collected rainwater, it is probably the sort of modest home Jesus' family would have owned. Many of Jesus' parables and sayings are redolent of the rural agricultural context in which he grew up. In their use of such themes as debt and landless labourers' search for work, they also reflect the hardship of many peasant farmers, at a time when large estates were depriving many smallholders and tenant farmers of their land.

According to the Gospel of Mark, Jesus was a 'carpenter' – this is the usual translation, but the Greek word is a rather vague term that could mean he worked in either wood or stone. According to the Gospel of Matthew, this was the trade of his father Joseph,

4. A home in Nazareth from the time of Jesus

and it is likely enough Jesus would have learned his trade from his father. It has often been thought that, as artisans, Jesus and his father would have been a cut above the average peasant farmer, but we should beware the anachronistic notion of a middle class. A huge gap separated the very small, very wealthy elite from the mass of ordinary people, who, by our standards, though not theirs, would be considered poor. An artisan would not necessarily have been better off than a relatively prosperous peasant farmer.

One intriguing piece of evidence suggests that Jesus may in fact have worked on the family farm as well as practising carpentry. Hegesippus, a 2nd-century writer, preserves the information that two grandsons of Jesus' brother Judas were peasant farmers sharing a farm whose precise size was remembered. This must have been the family smallholding in Nazareth. The fact that they owned it jointly indicates that this family still followed the rather old-fashioned practice of not dividing the farm but keeping it as the common property of the extended family. Since Joseph had to provide for at least seven children (Jesus, his four brothers, and two or more sisters), he may well have taken up carpentry only to supplement the inadequate produce of the family farm. For this purpose, there would have been enough work within Nazareth.

Galilee had only two cities, Sepphoris and Tiberias, respectively rebuilt and built by Herod Antipas, dependent for goods and services on the villages around. Sepphoris was only five miles from Nazareth, and doubtless Jesus had visited it. But that the cities had much cultural influence on the conservative society of rural Galilee seems unlikely. In religious practice, archaeological evidence (such as immersion baths for ritual purification and the absence of pig bones) shows that Galileans did not differ significantly from Judaeans. They observed Torah, though not necessarily in accordance with Pharisaic interpretation, and they went on pilgrimage to the Temple in Jerusalem, while not necessarily approving of the wealthy, priestly aristocracy who ran it. Until he was around 30 years of age, this was Jesus' world. Of his education, we know nothing, and can only surmise that he learned Hebrew, studied the Hebrew Scriptures intently, and listened to religious teachers, from whom he learned such forms of teaching as parables and aphorisms.

While Galilee was the scene of Jesus' formation, we should not exaggerate the extent to which it was the scene of Jesus' activity of teaching and healing. Mark's Gospel focuses largely on Galilee and on the short time Jesus spent in Jerusalem at the end of his life, but even Mark refers to journeys in the areas north of Galilee, in Judaea and in Jewish territory east of the Jordan river. Luke's Gospel, on the other hand, devotes less than six chapters to Jesus' activity in Galilee, compared with more than ten chapters set rather vaguely en route between Galilee and Jerusalem. From John's Gospel, we learn something at which the other Gospels only hint: that Jesus made several visits to Jerusalem and spent considerable periods of time there. Since John's Gospel is the most precise in matters of chronology and geography, there is reason to trust its claim that Jesus did not confine his activity to outlying parts of Jewish Palestine but also made his presence felt at the heart of the Jewish theocracy – the holy city and the Temple.

Messianism

The Hebrew word 'Messiah' (in Greek *Christos*, hence Jesus *Christ*) means 'anointed one'. A proper Jewish theocracy, as many Jews of this period imagined it, should have two 'anointed ones': a legitimate king descended from David and a legitimate high priest descended from Aaron and Zadok. The sectarian priests who wrote some of the Dead Sea Scrolls therefore expected two Messiahs, with the high priest in the dominant role. They also expected there to be a third figure, a prophet, with the function of communicating oracles from God, but this figure is never actually called an anointed one.

However, among the people generally, it was bound to be the royal Messiah of David who took centre stage, because the priority was liberation from Roman rule, and it was the new David who, like David of old, would lead the armies of Israel to military victory. The evidence of the Gospels is therefore credible that at the time of Jesus, there was a quite widespread expectation of a Davidic Messiah and that 'the Messiah' commonly referred to this figure. It was in this kind of role that some of Jesus' contemporaries cast him, and it was on the charge of being such a 'king of the Jews' that the Roman authorities had him executed.

An alternative scenario was based on the hope for a liberating event modelledon the Exodus from Egypt and the conquest of the land of Israel. This was the model that the celebration of the Temple festivals would have encouraged in the popular mind. Here the conquering hero would be a new Moses, or perhaps a new Joshua, and the hope for success would be focused especially on miraculous intervention by God, even if human arms were to play some part, as they did in the original conquest of the land. The expected leader might be called king (as Moses sometimes was) but more usually the prophet – not, in this case, an oracular prophet, but a prophet like Moses, a charismatic leader.

In the decades between Jesus and the great revolt, a number of pretenders to such a role appeared, typically leading their followers into the wilderness, where they promised a miraculous sign from God to authenticate them and to indicate that the time for liberation had come. But the possibility that already Jesus himself was mistakenly identified as such a figure seems likely. It was when he miraculously fed a large crowd in the wilderness, recalling Moses' provision of food to Israel in the wilderness, that he had to escape an attempt by the crowd to make him king. There was therefore more than one 'messianic' role into which his contemporaries could attempt to fit him.

5. Map of Palestine in the time of Jesus

John the Baptist

When early Christians told the story of Jesus, they seem habitually to have begun, not with Jesus himself, but with the Jewish prophet known as John the Baptist. John was a fiery preacher, reminiscent of Elijah, with a probably unexpected message, though one that had much precedent among the prophets of the Hebrew Bible. He announced not the imminent liberation of Israel but the judgement of God impending on Israel for their sin. As far as our sources tell us, he had nothing to say about the Romans, though he did criticize Herod Antipas. He called people into the wilderness, not in order to prepare to re-conquer the land, but in order to immerse them in the river as a ritual of repentance. Only by national repentance could Israel escape the coming wrath of God. John's baptism was a last opportunity for a rebellious nation to put itself right with God.

John attracted huge crowds to undergo baptism, and his disciples included some who also became the first disciples of Jesus. John denied speculation that he might be some sort of messianic figure, and seems to have cast himself rather in the role of forerunner to a greater figure who would come as the agent of God's judgement. It was in the context of expectations raised by John that Jesus' public activity began. These expectations might be bleak, but they also meant that at last the great turning point in Israel's story might be imminent.

Jesus himself went to John for baptism and seems to have stayed some time with him. At Jesus' baptism, he and John shared a vision in which Jesus received his messianic anointing with the Spirit of God and heard himself called the beloved son of God. Whatever Jesus might have thought of his vocation before this point, this experience finally gave him the mission from God that he now set out to accomplish.

While Jesus' message, a joyful proclamation of good news, would contrast sharply with the doom-laden prophecies of John, Jesus shared with John one extremely important perspective. Like John, he paid little attention to the Romans, because his priority was the renewal of God's own people. Among the major Jewish parties, it was perhaps the Pharisees, with their programme for national holiness, that the movement Jesus started and led most resembled, and this is why it was with the Pharisees that he most often clashed. Theirs were alternative visions of the renewal of Israel.

Chapter 4
Enacting the kingdom of God

God's rule is arriving

In the modern period, Jesus has often been seen as a teacher of
ethics or a social reformer. These views are not completely
mistaken. There is a good deal of material in the Gospels to support
them. But they are seriously inadequate. They focus in too modern
and humanistic a way on how people should live. But what fired
Jesus' mission was his experience of *God*. What mattered to him,
first and foremost, was the God of Israel, God's love for his people
and his world, and what God was doing for his people and his
world. How God's people should live also mattered profoundly, but
it would never have occurred to Jesus that one could get that right
without appreciating what God was like and what God was doing.

The first three Gospels, the Synoptics, make it abundantly clear
that at the heart of all that Jesus said and did lay what he called
'the kingdom of God'. This translation is the familiar one, but 'rule'
might be closer than 'kingdom' to what Jesus meant. The term is
dynamic and refers primarily to the activity of God. But, in Jesus'
usage, 'the kingdom of God' is also something one can 'enter', and
in this case, it designates the sphere of God's rule, which in
English we would call his 'kingdom' or 'realm'. So we need to bear
in mind both dimensions – active rule and territorial kingdom – if
we are to do justice to Jesus' usage.

Jesus' Jewish contemporaries would have had no difficulty in understanding broadly what Jesus meant by 'the kingdom of God'. Though the Hebrew Bible does not use this phrase, it does speak frequently of God as king, of God's throne, and of God reigning over Israel and the world. From his heavenly throne, God rules his whole creation, while from his throne in his Temple in Jerusalem, he reigns over his own special people, Israel. In these senses, God's kingdom already exists.

With these aspects of God's rule, Jesus had no quarrel, but in his own talk of God's kingdom he was not simply affirming that God is king. He was speaking of something new that was arriving. He was picking up the sense in which, for the Jewish Scriptures and later Jewish literature, the fullness of God's rule was something still to be expected in the future. At present, God's sovereignty is ultimately supreme, but it is not acknowledged by the nations, who worship other gods instead. At present, God's active rule is contested by the forces of evil, supernatural and human, that are responsible for such wrongs as violence, sickness, injustice, oppression, and even death. The people of Israel therefore looked for a time when God's rule would be universally acknowledged and would prevail over all evil. Jesus taught his disciples to pray for this:

> May your name be sanctified,
> may your kingdom come,
> may your will be done
> on earth as it is in heaven.

The meaning is that in heaven, where the angels worship God and carry out his will, God's kingdom already exists in its perfection, but this is not yet true on earth.

In such a prayer for the coming of God's kingdom, all of Jesus' Jewish hearers would readily – even eagerly and with passion – have joined. But what was distinctive about Jesus' message was, in the words with which the Gospels sum it up: 'the kingdom of God is close at hand'. It was already arriving. The powerful and transformative rule of God was taking effect in a new way. Israel's hopes were being realized, God's promises fulfilled.

For understanding Jesus, the timing of the kingdom is important, but the character of the kingdom is even more important. Jesus evidently did not think that the kingdom was coming all at once. There was a process. From its small beginnings in Jesus' own teaching and activity, the kingdom would ultimately blossom into universal reality. Jesus was aware that what he identified as the arrival of the kingdom hardly began to match up to the dimensions of Israel's hopes for the future.

In one of his parables, he compared the kingdom to a mustard seed, which was proverbially known as the smallest of all seeds. With his customary hyperbole, Jesus said that it grows into 'the greatest of all shrubs' with branches in which the birds can nest. There was precedent in the Hebrew Bible for picturing God's universal rule as a great tree, planted in the centre of the world, and covering the whole earth with its branches for the benefit of all creatures. According to Jesus' parable, this greatest of all trees had its beginnings in the smallest of all seeds. In Jesus' own teaching and activity, insignificant though they might seem in the grand perspective of world history, God really was sowing the seed of his coming kingdom.

But if the arrival of the kingdom was so unimpressive, what reason might there be for recognizing it as the coming of God's kingdom? The answer to this lies in Jesus' understanding of the character of the kingdom. What is God's rule like? For some of Jesus' contemporaries, God's priority must surely be the liberation of his people from the yoke of the Roman oppressor. He must establish his own sole rule over his holy people by defeating those who had no right to rule them. If this were seen to be happening, God's kingdom might be said to be arriving. But for Jesus, there

were other priorities. He saw the kingdom arriving in the sorts of
things he was doing: bringing God's healing and forgiveness into
the lives of people he met, reaching out to those who were pushed
to the margins of God's people, gathering a community in which
service would replace status. These are the sorts of things that
happen when God rules.

Such a vision of the coming rule of God Jesus found in the
prophecies of Israel's prophets. But it was even more deeply
rooted in his understanding of the God of the Hebrew Bible. What
God's rule is like corresponds to what God is like. So our account
of Jesus' understanding of the kingdom must take us, in due
course, to his understanding of the God of the kingdom.

To his disciples, Jesus spoke of the extraordinary moment of
history they were witnessing:

> Blessed are the eyes that see what you see! For I tell you that many
> prophets and kings desired to see what you see, but did not see it,
> and to hear what you hear, but did not hear it.
>
> (Luke 10:23–24)

The kingdom of God was coming because Jesus himself enacted it
and proclaimed it. What he did and what he said were both
important, and in our quest to understand more of the character
of God's rule as Jesus saw it, we shall consider first what he did.

The healing power of God's rule

Jesus' public life as an itinerant healer and teacher seems to have
lasted not much more than two years. This is a remarkably short
period in which to have made the impact he did. Probably we
should distinguish the impact he made on his disciples, who
shared his life and committed his teaching to memory, from the
impact he made on people generally. The key to the latter was his
reputation as a healer.

Jesus healed people of all kinds of disabilities and diseases. He also exorcized demons. In that society, demons could be held responsible for disabilities and diseases, but the Gospels rarely allude to such a belief. Exorcisms differed from healings because they expelled the demons from people whom demons had taken over and held in their power. Sometimes the symptoms were such

6. Jesus heals a haemorrhaging woman (catacomb fresco)

as we would attribute to mental illness. The demon-possessed were not, it seems, regarded as wicked people voluntarily in league with evil, but as innocent victims of powers of evil they were unable to resist.

Jesus' exorcisms had the special value of dramatizing his power to overcome the forces of evil and to rescue those who were enslaved to them. He said:

> If it is by the finger of God that I cast out demons, then the kingdom of God has come to you.
>
> (Luke 11:20)

Though Jesus was by no means the only Jewish exorcist, so far as we know he was the only one to link his exorcisms with the new thing that God was doing: the coming of the kingdom. For this to have been at all plausible, he must have been an exceptionally successful exorcist, something which is also suggested by the fact that other exorcists apparently took to using Jesus' name as the word of power with which they drove out demons. Jesus' success as an exorcist provoked his enemies to find an alternative explanation for it. They said that Jesus was in league with the powers of evil and was himself possessed by the prince of the demons.

Notable among the people Jesus is said to have healed were disabled beggars: the blind, the deaf, and the lame. Such people found it hard to find work and, unless they belonged to a wealthy family, were obliged to beg. They probably did better than disabled people in much of the ancient world, because Jews regarded charity to the poor as an important duty. But begging was not an enviable lifestyle, and, by healing these people, Jesus gave them back their dignity and a place in society.

This was even more emphatically the case with people suffering from leprosy. (The word probably covered a variety of serious skin diseases, not only what we call leprosy, that is, Hansen's disease.) These people were obliged to keep away from the rest of society, not because their illness was regarded as infectious, but because they were defined as 'impure' (or 'unclean') in a religious sense. (We shall discuss this concept of cultic impurity later.) So that other people could recognize them and keep well clear of them, they were supposed to dress in rags and to shout out 'unclean' wherever they went. Jesus not only healed them, but also, in a gesture that surely meant much to them, healed them by touching them.

It is evident that in these 'deeds of power' (as the Synoptic Gospels call them) Jesus restored people to more than physical health. He also restored social relationships, re-integrating people into the society of God's people Israel. We should also remember that many of these people – the disabled, people with leprosy, and the demon-possessed – were barred, by their conditions, from the earthly presence of God in his Temple in Jerusalem. This did not put them outside the loving concern of God, but it did distance them from the symbolic heart of Israel's special relationship with their God. Jesus' healings were for them an experience of the God who was reaching out to abolish that distance. In the fullest sense, these healings were holistic.

The Gospels tell of an occasion when John the Baptist, then in prison, wanted to know whether Jesus was really the expected Messiah, as he had thought when he baptized him. Perhaps he was puzzled that Jesus was not doing what John thought the Messiah would do: bring down God's judgement on the wicked and unrepentant in Israel. So John sent some of his disciples to ask Jesus, 'Are you the one who is to come, or are we to wait for another?' Jesus did not answer this question directly. He rarely answered that kind of question, because he did not want to be saddled with whatever ideas the questioner had about the Messiah. Instead, he pointed to what was happening before the eyes of the questioners:

Go and tell John what you see and hear: the blind receive their
sight, the lame walk, the lepers are cleansed, the deaf hear, the dead
are raised, and the poor have good news brought to them. (Matthew
11:2–5)

What sort of Messiah you expected depended a lot on which
biblical prophecies you focused on. For those who knew the
Scriptures well, as John the Baptist did, Jesus' reply echoed
passages in the later chapters of Isaiah (35:5–6; 61:1). Jesus was
inviting John to recognize that the sorts of things that were
happening in Jesus' ministry were the sorts of things the prophet
said would accompany God's coming to rule. As to who Jesus was,
John could draw his own conclusions.

It has sometimes been suggested that the stories of Jesus' miracles
were invented on the basis of the prophecies. But one reason why
this cannot be the case can be found in precisely this passage
where the prophecies are cited. None of the prophecies say
anything about lepers or anything that could be interpreted as
referring to lepers. The lepers are in the list not because the
prophecies mention them, but because as a matter of fact they
were prominent among the people Jesus healed.

We should not suppose that Jesus simply acted out a programme
set for him by his reading of prophetic Scriptures. Jesus was
moved by the suffering he encountered, the manifold forms of
deprivation and diminishment of life he saw all around him in the
villages of Galilee. He was moved by the faith of the crowds of
people who brought their sick loved ones to him. The power of
healing they drew from him he understood to be the power of the
divine compassion. He saw his healings as signs of the kingdom of
God because they were so obviously acts of the God whom Jesus
understood as above all loving and compassionate. Jesus was
enacting the kingdom by enacting the divine compassion. What he
saw in the prophecies was that precisely such outpourings of divine
compassion were to be expected when Israel's God came to establish

his kingdom. It was not the way everyone read the Scriptures, but it was what leapt out of the page when Jesus read them.

Another feature of Jesus' healings that could not simply be read out of the prophecies was that he required faith – on the part either of those who wanted to be healed or of those who brought them to be healed. The Gospels note the rather embarrassing fact that, when Jesus made a return visit to his home town, Nazareth, he was able to heal only a very few sick people, because he found so little faith there. When Jesus said to people he had healed, 'Your faith has made you well', we might suppose he meant he had done nothing but trigger some kind of self-healing power in the sick person. But this would be a mistake because 'faith' meant trusting God – or the healing power of God that Jesus made available. (We need not distinguish trust in God from trust in Jesus in such cases.) Faith opened people to the power of divine compassion that came from outside themselves. But it is significant that Jesus did not treat the sick as mere passive recipients of healing. He sought their engagement in their own healing. He made their experience part of their relationship with God.

Enacting the kingdom at table

In one of his deft, short parables, Jesus compared those who resisted his message to uncooperative and peevish children:

> They are like children sitting in the marketplace and calling to one another,
> 'We played the flute for you, and you did not dance;
> we sang a dirge, and you did not weep'.

(Luke 7:12, altered)

One group of children complains that the other group wouldn't join in their games. Whether they proposed a happy game (dancing to the flute) or a sad one (pretending to mourn), it was the same. The others refused to play.

Jesus applies the story to the reception that John the Baptist and he himself had received:

> For John the Baptist has come eating no bread and drinking no
>   wine,
> and you say, 'He has a demon';
> the Son of Man [Jesus himself] came eating and drinking,
> and you say, 'Look, a glutton and a drunkard,
> a friend of tax collectors and sinners'.

(Luke 7:13-14)

The fiery prophet John the Baptist had adopted an ascetic lifestyle appropriate to his stern message of coming judgement and the need for repentance. Jesus' lifestyle was very different. He fraternized with all sorts of people and shared meals with them.

The words Jesus here quotes from his opponents offer a fascinating insight into how he was perceived by some people. The two charges of indulgence in food and drink and associating with notorious sinners are really just one: Jesus partied with the wrong sort of people.

In that society, it mattered a lot whom you chose to eat with. In all traditional societies, meals do not just satisfy hunger in enjoyable ways; they have richly symbolic meanings. By eating with some but not with others, people may reinforce or establish social boundaries. But in Jewish society in the time of Jesus, such demarcations between in-groups and out-groups were not arbitrary; they reflected a pervasive preoccupation with holiness.

The Pharisees were particularly concerned with ritual purity and with eating their meals in purity. Food had to have been properly tithed, hands must be properly washed, and people should not sit down with others in a state of contagious impurity. Some scholars have thought that the accusations against Jesus have this kind of background. Jesus was careless about purity rules and shared meals with ordinary people who couldn't be bothered with the niceties of Pharisaic purity. But holiness was a matter not just of purity, but also of morality, and associating too closely with flagrantly immoral people could endanger one's own moral integrity. One didn't have to be a Pharisee to think that.

The prime example of the kind of sinners Jesus befriended were the tax collectors. Tax collectors were generally ostracized not because of their ritual impurity, but for much more serious reasons. They were Jews working for the Roman overlords (or for Rome's puppet king Herod Antipas), and they made their own living out of collecting more than the taxes and pocketing the difference. No doubt they often made a very good living. It was for greed and extortion at the expense of their fellow Jews, as well as for working for the hated Roman Empire, that they were ostracized.

The example of the tax collectors shows that the 'sinners' Jesus befriended were not just careless about ritual purity, but people who flagrantly broke the moral requirements of God's law, the Torah. Elsewhere prostitutes are also mentioned. The problem for Jesus' opponents was really that he ate with all sorts of people. He accepted invitations to dine with Pharisees, but also with tax collectors and the sorts of people who associated with tax collectors. He seems, in fact, to have made a special point of doing the latter. In the case of Zacchaeus, for example, a rather high-ranking and so an especially wealthy tax collector, Jesus invited himself to be Zacchaeus's house guest.

Did Jesus not expect such people to reform? His own demanding moral teaching surely implies that he did, and Zacchaeus, for one, did so. But Jesus did not wait for such people to repent before sharing meals with them. This is what distinguished his practice from Jewish leaders who would not have denied that people like tax collectors could repent and obtain forgiveness from God. To put it simply, Jesus did not keep his distance from anyone who needed the love of God, whether they needed liberation from demons, healing of sickness, or forgiveness of sin. This was his mission from God, and it left him no room for protecting himself from being contaminated by the impurity or immorality of others.

While Jesus no doubt expected the likes of tax collectors to turn their lives around, it is notable that he does not seem to have denounced them in the way he denounced some of the religious leaders. He didn't need to. Everyone knew they were sinners, and they knew it themselves. In the story Jesus told of a Pharisee and a tax collector praying in the Temple, the tax collector knows only too well his need of God's forgiveness, but the Pharisee, priding himself on his exemplary religious rectitude, is unable to acknowledge his failings. What Jesus denounced was the arrogance and hypocrisy of people who set themselves up as models of piety and misled others, while themselves transgressing the central requirements of Torah in subtle ways that deceived even themselves. They needed stronger medicine than the tax collectors and prostitutes who, as Jesus put it, were entering the kingdom ahead of them.

We learn more about Jesus' meals from the contrast he himself drew between his own approach and that of John the Baptist. Unlike his predecessor, Jesus came with the good news of the kingdom and he celebrated this in his meals. They were not solemn affairs, but joyful celebrations of the coming of the kingdom. Whereas the disciples of John, like many other Jews, practised a strict regime of fasting, Jesus' disciples puzzled them by not fasting. But for Jesus' disciples to fast, he said, would be as inappropriate as fasting at a wedding. While the Pharisees turned ordinary meals into a practice of ritual holiness, Jesus turned ordinary meals into a practice of the coming of God's kingdom.

They were especially suitable for this purpose because a familiar image of the messianic age to come was the great banquet that God would host, where all his faithful people would sit together with the patriarchs Abraham, Isaac, and Jacob. In Jesus' practice of meal fellowship, he, so to speak, goes ahead with the love of God to welcome to the banquet everyone who will accept the invitation. Eating with Jesus was virtually tantamount to entering the kingdom and sitting at table with the patriarchs.

The kingdom belongs to the poor

When Jesus passed through Jericho on the way to Jerusalem, on his last visit to the city, a blind beggar at the back of the crowds that thronged the route managed to get Jesus' attention. His blindness healed, he eagerly joined the followers of Jesus. Mark's Gospel tells us his name: Bartimaeus. No doubt he became well known in the early Christian movement in Jerusalem. Mark may have got the story straight from his mouth. Bartimaeus must have been one of those many Palestinian Jews whose personal name was an extremely common one (such as Simon or Judah), too common to be of any use in identifying him. Following a common practice, he was therefore known by his patronymic. 'Bar' is the Aramaic word for 'son', while Timaeus was a Greek name only rarely used among Palestinian Jews, which therefore served very well to identify Bartimaeus. These comments on the name are worth making because they show that names of such people in the Gospels are historically plausible. (Jews outside Palestine followed different naming practices.)

For an individual beggar to appear in the literature of Greco-Roman antiquity is a very rare occurrence. For an individual beggar to appear with a name is almost unique. The histories and biographies of the period, which the Gospels most resemble in terms of literary genre, are peopled predominantly by the wealthy elite, since these were considered the people who made history happen. To a large extent, it was the wealthy elite who read such literature (though it might well be a slave who read it aloud to them), and they despised the ordinary people. The latter appear

7. A 1st-century fishing boat from the Sea of Galilee

mostly in such literature as the anonymous conglomerate, 'the crowd', for whom the authors regularly display contempt.

In such a literary context, the Gospels are an extraordinary exception. The many individuals who appear in their pages are spread across the whole social scale. There are members of the elite (such as the Jerusalem aristocracy) and the retainers of the elite (such as centurions and tax collectors). But far more of these individuals belong to the ordinary people (peasant farmers, fishermen, artisans), who made up the large mass of the population. Even more remarkable is the generous representation given by the Gospels to people belonging to the two categories that formed the lowest rungs on the social ladder. One of these is 'the poor', in the sense in which the Gospels mean it, that is, referring not to the ordinary people who had at least a stable income at subsistence level, barring bad harvests, sickness, and other misfortunes, but to the really destitute. These were the people who had no reliable means of support, but had to depend largely on the charity of others. They included the poor widow Jesus commended when she put all she had, just two small coins, into the Temple collection box. They also included the many disabled beggars Jesus restored to health, dignity, and a place in society.

Such people were doubtless pitied by the ordinary people, not least because only a narrow line, easily crossed in the downward direction, separated the destitute from those whose place among the self-supporting was rather precarious. But the dregs of the earth were the outcasts, who for one reason or another were excluded from society altogether: lepers, those possessed by demons (at least if they were uncontrollable, like the man in the Gospels known as Legion), prostitutes, bandits, and criminals. In the perspective of the ordinary people, doubtless tax collectors also belonged to this category. Not a few members of these outcast groups appear in the Gospels, along with a number of Gentiles and Samaritans (an Israelite group disowned by the Jews). The destitute and the outcasts were only a very small proportion of the population, as were the elite. It is remarkable that we meet as many of them in the Gospels as we do of the elite and their retainers. Of course, the crowds that flocked to Jesus for healing and to hear him teach would have been made up mainly of the ordinary people and some of the destitute.

These facts about the social status of the characters in the Gospels reflect the realities of Jesus' social world and the priorities of his mission. He himself was a man of the people. He did have disciples and sympathizers among the elite (Joanna, a Galilean aristocrat; Joseph of Arimathea and Nicodemus, both members of the high priest's ruling council), though he could be very critical of the ruling elite, and he certainly had no policy for reforming Jewish society from the top down. He operated rather at the grassroots. The first disciples he called, the core of his movement, were mostly fishermen. But he and his itinerant followers themselves voluntarily adopted the way of life and status of the destitute, lacking permanent abode, with no earnings to support them. The generous representation of destitute people and outcasts in the Gospels reflects the way in which Jesus seems not only to have attracted such people, in search of healing or forgiveness and acceptance, but also deliberately to have sought them out. It was part of his understanding of his mission to pay attention to those whom most people brushed aside or scorned. It was to them especially that the kingdom of God belonged.

Renewing the people of God

One of the most important of Jesus' symbolic acts was his selection of twelve of his disciples for a special vocation. The number twelve could not fail to evoke the twelve tribes of Israel. Jesus' twelve could not have been literally drawn from each of the twelve tribes, because we know that they included two pairs of brothers, but symbolically they would certainly have recalled the ideal constitution of Israel as a people of twelve tribes.

This symbolism enables us to recognize two key aspects of the way Jesus understood his mission from God. In the first place, it was a mission to God's people Israel, all twelve tribes of them. Like John the Baptist before him, Jesus preached an urgent message to the whole nation, calling on them to repent, to turn to God, to reorder their lives in such a way as to be the nation God had chosen them to be, the renewed Israel of the messianic age. Although, like John, Jesus did foresee judgement for the unrepentant, the distinctive character of his mission lay in his conviction that the kingdom of his was already within reach, not yet as judgement, but as the power of God's grace, mercy, compassion, healing, and forgiveness. This gave him a special concern for the 'lost sheep' of God's flock–the people who were in one way or another marginal or excluded. We have mentioned some of them: the beggars, the demon-possessed, the notorious sinners. With the coming of the kingdom, such people were not to be left aside, but welcomed in. Since the kingdom was arriving as divine healing and compassion, it had, as it were, special relevance to these people. Comparing his role with that of a medical practitioner, Jesus said, 'Those who are well have no need of a physician, but those who are sick.'

The second aspect of Jesus' mission that his appointment of the twelve highlights is this: as well as throwing open the arms of God's mercy to welcome people into the kingdom, Jesus set about establishing a community of disciples that would be the nucleus of the renewed people. The precedent in the Hebrew Bible for Jesus' twelve was not so much the twelve patriarchs, the ancestors of the tribes, but the twelve princes of the tribes, whom Moses appointed to head up the people of Israel in the wilderness after the Exodus. Jesus' twelve disciples were the leaders of the Israel of the new exodus. By accompanying Jesus at all times, they were to learn from him how to continue his own mission: to heal and to exorcize, to bring the good news of the kingdom to the destitute and the outcasts.

However, we should not imagine that this specially selected group of twelve were the only disciples of Jesus or the only ones that shared his itinerant ministry. Luke's Gospel, especially, provides a broader picture of many other disciples, most of whom remain anonymous, but some of whom are named and appear as quite prominent figures. The twelve had a special symbolic role, but many others also accompanied Jesus on his journeys around the country. No doubt the size and composition of the large group of disciples that travelled around with Jesus varied from time to time, and there are indications that the number declined in the latter part of his ministry. Some are likely to have been disappointed that Jesus did not turn out to be the kind of Messiah they hoped. But up to and including his final visit to Jerusalem, Jesus seems always to have had with him a group of disciples, male and female, that was larger than the twelve.

Of special importance, alongside the twelve, were a group of women disciples. The twelve had to be male because of the

scriptural precedent they evoked, but Luke's Gospel in particular
stresses that several women also accompanied Jesus from an early
stage of his ministry right up until his death. The best known is
Mary Magdalene. Another was Joanna, wife of a high-ranking
official at the court of Herod Antipas. She must have been one of
the women who, we are told, helped to support Jesus and the
other disciples financially. (Most of the male disciples had left
behind families for whom they were the main providers and could
hardly have been able to put much into the disciples' common
purse.) But it was not for this reason that they were included
among Jesus' followers. Had they been only patrons of Jesus'
movement, as some wealthy and influential women were of the
Pharisees, they could have stayed at home and spared themselves
the scandal of sharing the life of these vagrant men. They were
with Jesus to learn, just as the male disciples were.

For such itinerant disciples who left their homes and families to
be with Jesus all the time, Jesus' demands were very stringent.
They had to be totally committed to him and the cause of the
kingdom (the two are not distinguishable in Jesus' words in this
connection). To a would-be disciple who wanted first to bury his
father, Jesus said, 'Follow me, and let the dead bury the dead'.
Seemingly, the urgent importance of the kingdom of God here
takes precedence even over one of the Ten Commandments (the
Commandment to honour one's father and mother). Jesus made
the same point a general rule when he said that no one could be
his disciple if they loved a family member more than him. This
kind of claim makes sense only if Jesus held that the commitment
of a disciple to him was a form of devotion to God, which alone
could take precedence over duties to family members. In the
situation of the arrival of the kingdom, nothing could be more
important.

The disciples of Jesus were engaged in a very demanding
participation in his own mission. They were also, in their life
together, to model the kind of society the renewed Israel would be,

or, to put it another way, what a society living fully under God's rule would be like. This is of considerable importance for recognizing the distinctiveness of Jesus' understanding of the kingdom, but an account of it must be left to the next chapter.

As well as disciples who accompanied him in his travels around the land of Israel, Jesus also had adherents and sympathizers who stayed in their homes. Some of these provided hospitality for Jesus and the disciples, as did the family of siblings, Martha, Mary, and Lazarus, who lived near Jerusalem and hosted Jesus often enough for them to become some of his closest friends. In one of the stories about them, Mary is portrayed as the exemplary disciple, sitting at Jesus' feet attending to his teaching. To judge from the hugely expensive perfume with which Mary anointed Jesus, the family were quite well to do. Jesus must have had many such stay-at-home supporters, and occasionally the Gospels actually call such people disciples. But it is quite unclear what discipleship required for them. Despite the characteristically extreme language in which Jesus speaks of discipleship, he seems to have recognized that not all who responded to his message could be expected to become homeless vagrants.

Even this wider circle of disciples, however, fell far short of the response to his message that Jesus must have hoped for from the people at large. Huge crowds flocked to receive healing and to listen to his preaching, but in the long run most were evidently not willing to undergo the radical change of heart he demanded. Some of his sayings, presumably from a relatively late stage of his ministry, express deep disappointment and sadness over this. But he does not seem to have concluded that the 'little flock' of his disciples would be the only fruit of his mission, for he continued, up until his death, to train his disciples to extend his mission.

Finally, this is the context in which we should consider what Jesus thought about the world beyond Israel. If Jesus thought the kingdom of God was within reach, he could not have confined it to

Israel, for the prophecies promised the earth. His own mission to Israel was a necessary first step. The renewal of God's own people had to come first because, in the divine strategy, it was by means of his own people that the knowledge of the true God was to reach the rest of the nations. So it is quite plausible that Jesus envisaged his disciples taking the good news out into all the world.

One of the few stories of encounter between Jesus and non-Jews offers an intriguing insight into Jesus' sense of his mission. It is located in Phoenicia, the coastal area to the northwest of Galilee, to which Jesus once travelled, perhaps to reach Jews who lived in the area. A Gentile woman whose daughter was possessed by a demon came to ask Jesus to liberate her from it. Jesus' first response is almost rudely negative: 'Let the children be fed first, for it is not fair to take the children's food and to throw it to the dogs.' With the word 'first', Jesus indicates that the Gentiles' time will come, but his mission to Jews takes priority. The term 'dogs' was the common Jewish word for Gentiles, comparing the pariah dogs that roamed the streets and scavenged anything with the cultic impurity of the non-Jew. Jesus perhaps deliberately softens the image, referring instead to the household dogs, kept as guard dogs, who are fed on the family's leftovers. The woman's response is witty as well as insistent: 'Sir, even the dogs under the table eat the children's crumbs.' She proved a match for Jesus' dexterity with images, and he must have been impressed. She actually afforded him a fresh insight into his mission. While it *was* directed to Israel, this was no reason why he should not meet the request of a Gentile who actually approached him in faith, since to do so would not deprive Jews of anything. God's compassionate provision was abundant enough to overflow to Gentiles even now.

The kingdom of God in the Gospel of John

One of the many differences between the Gospel of John and the other three Gospels is that, whereas in the other Gospels the phrase 'the kingdom of God' (or 'the kingdom of heaven') is frequently on Jesus' lips, in John it occurs only twice. These two occurrences are at the beginning of Jesus' conversation with Nicodemus, but a reading of the whole conversation shows that Jesus does not drop the topic of the kingdom of God but uses for it the alternative term 'eternal life'. Whereas he first speaks of seeing the kingdom and entering the kingdom, he goes on to speak of having eternal life. The author is telling us that he knows Jesus regularly spoke of the kingdom of God, but in his own report and interpretation of Jesus' teaching, he has preferred the term 'eternal life'. In fact, this was by no means an innovation. In the Synoptic Gospels also, Jesus sometimes speaks of 'eternal life' or just 'life', using these phrases interchangeably with 'the kingdom of God'. John's usage in this case resembles other cases where he has taken up an expression or a topic that occurs only occasionally in the teaching of Jesus in the other Gospels and has made it a frequent usage or topic in his own Gospel.

John's preference for 'eternal life' does rather shift the focus from what God is doing to the content of what God gives. But 'eternal life' is no less oriented to God than is 'the kingdom of God', since in this Gospel eternal life is the life that has its source in God. Though it is to be contrasted with the mortal life that runs out in death, it is far from being mere never-ending existence. It is the fullness of life in relationship with God, life to the nth degree, a comprehensive term for all the blessings God has to give humanity. Jesus' mission is to make it available, as Jesus in this Gospel says: 'I came that they may have life, and have it abundantly.'

Just as in the Synoptic Gospels, Jesus' acts of healing are signs of the presence of the kingdom of God, not simply because they are miraculous, but also because they display the healing compassion of God that characterizes the kingdom, so in John's Gospel Jesus' healing miracles, which this Gospel regularly calls 'signs', signify the eternal life that Jesus brings. This focus on eternal life explains John's particular selection of miracle stories, of which he has far fewer than the other Gospels. All have to do with life: Jesus restores impaired life, sustains life with food, even brings back to life a man who had been dead three days. These signs, in which Jesus gives mortal life, signify the much greater gift of eternal life that comes through his own rising to eternal life through death. The miracle at the wedding at Cana may not seem at first to fit this pattern, but, against the background of the Jewish image of the messianic banquet, the large quantity of excellent wine Jesus provides signifies the abundant and enhanced life, the extravagant fullness of life that Jesus came to bring. In the story of the healing of the blind man, the symbolism points to seeing the light, but in this Gospel light and life are closely connected. The man receives his sight so that he may walk in the light of life. This brief sketch of the signs in John's Gospel provides an illustration of the way this Gospel reports events of Jesus' history, much as the other Gospels do, understands them in ways that certainly have continuity with the other Gospels, but also goes further in its attempt to explicate their full significance.

Chapter 5
Teaching the kingdom of God

Style of teaching

Jesus favoured indirect communication. Sometimes, of course, he spoke directly and straightforwardly, but much more often he used forms of speech that appeal to the imagination or provoke thought. He asks questions without giving answers. He regularly talks about one thing in terms of another – through metaphors, similes, analogies, and stories that mean more than they say. For example, Jesus could have said, 'The kingdom of God is something of such supreme value that you ought to be willing to give up everything else in order to attain it.' In fact, he told a short story about a merchant who, in his quest for fine pearls, one day came upon an extremely valuable one and sold everything else in order to be able to buy it. Jesus could have said, 'Someone who wants to be my disciple must be resolute and single-minded about it.' In fact, he said, 'No one who puts a hand to the plough and looks back is fit for the kingdom of God.'

Even apparently straightforward sayings may turn out to be hyperbole or irony. Jesus often teaches by instancing a shockingly extreme example: if someone wants your coat, strip naked and give him everything you're wearing. There are paradoxes and riddles, such as: 'Whoever seeks to gain their life will lose it, but whoever loses their life will keep it.' He gives people figurative labels: Herod is 'that fox', his disciples are his 'little flock', his leading disciple is 'the Rock', Pharisees are a 'brood of vipers', Jesus himself is 'the Son of man'. His use of this enigmatic form of self-reference may be an extended riddle. Certainly, Jesus speaks of his destiny in riddles: a cup he must drink, a baptism with which he must be baptized. He paints the future in the vivid colours of scriptural imagery: 'they will see the Son of man coming on clouds with great power and glory'.

Along with Jesus' forms of indirect communication in words, we should also include his indirect communication by significant actions. We have already noticed the rich symbolism of the meals he shares with others. There are many other examples. Sometimes an action illustrates what he says: he takes a child in his arms and tells his disciples that they must become like children if they are to enter the kingdom. Sometimes the action speaks for itself, as when he rides into Jerusalem on a donkey. Perhaps the most potent of all Jesus' symbolic actions was when he washed the feet of his disciples, taking a role that was almost exclusively that of a slave.

There is probably no one explanation for Jesus' overwhelming preference for forms of indirect communication. But a common feature is that indirect communication creates a pause for thought between what is said and the hearer's realization of what is meant. The pause may be momentary, as a striking illustration hits home – with shock or with delight or with a sense of fresh recognition. Or the pause may give time for a message to sink in. Or the pause may be indefinitely long, as when the hearer goes away still puzzling over the point of a story or pondering the significance of a weighty saying. The pause may create a space in which the hearer can re-consider an accepted view, see something in a different light, have cherished opinions challenged. When a hearer is absorbed in a story, an unexpected truth may creep up on them and take them by surprise.

The material for Jesus' comparisons and parables comes from the ordinary life of 1st-century Palestine. He does draw on images familiar from the Hebrew Bible (such as God as the shepherd of his people, Israel as God's vineyard) and can make specific reference to passages and stories in the Hebrew Bible (such as Jonah or commandments of the Torah), but for the most part, when not debating with religious leaders, he does not engage in learned exegesis of Scripture. Though his thought is profoundly rooted in the Hebrew Bible, most of his figurative comparisons seem freshly minted from the world that he and his hearers knew well. In the case of the narrative parables, there are striking similarities with – as well as differences from – parables of the Jewish rabbis that date from a much later period. Jesus must have drawn on a stock of storytelling motifs that continued to inform Jewish religious teaching down to the time of the rabbis. He is not likely to have simply taken over existing stories, but, like every good storyteller, would often have developed his own stories from current motifs. One revealing difference from the parables of the rabbis is that in them the character with whom God is compared is always a king, whereas this is true of only two of Jesus' parables. Instead, there are landowners, householders, and fathers – authority figures closer to the ordinary experience of Jesus' hearers. The situations portrayed in the parables and other sayings are notably small scale and everyday – a feature that not only made them accessible and meaningful to ordinary people in a rural context, but surely also reflects Jesus' understanding of the kingdom of God as something that was beginning to take shape in local and seemingly unimpressive ways.

Among the sayings of Jesus, it is the narrative parables that have received most attention. There are about forty of them in the Synoptic Gospels (the exact number depends on some debatable issues of exact definition), and a mere half dozen others in extra-canonical literature. They range from very short narratives (like the merchant and the pearl, cited above) to relatively long ones, such as the well-known stories of the Prodigal Son and the Good Samaritan. Even the latter are short, as stories go, but none of them wastes words. They say only what is necessary for the point the story makes. Many are nevertheless engaging stories that draw their hearers into them, which is no doubt one reason for their popularity and influence. The stories are not usually predictable, though in some cases predictability is essential to the effect. Though they portray ordinary life, they are often not fully realistic, making their point by hyperbole or surprise. Good rules for understanding them are to let the story make its impact as a story before seeking its message and to attend especially to the way the story takes a surprising turn, when it does. Often, the improbable or shocking turn the story takes gives it a message that subverts and reverses common attitudes or expectations. But not all do this, and Jesus was not a revolutionary thinker in every respect.

In general, the parables do not teach broad moral lessons or truths about God and the world. Most are stories about the kingdom. They are about the new thing that Jesus believed God was doing in the midst of his people Israel. Thus, for example, the well-known parable of the Prodigal Son is not simply about the forgiving love of God for all who repent, but more specifically about what God was doing in Jesus' mission to actualize the forgiving love of God in his outreach especially to those of God's people who might seem to have strayed furthest from it.

Compared with the narrative parables, the short aphorisms of Jesus, of which there are many more, generally receive less attention. Readers with modern reading habits tend to skim quickly through them, whereas they are meant to be paused on and pondered. Sometimes they encapsulate a feature of Jesus' teaching in memorable form that will sink into the mind and influence practice, as in the case of Jesus' simple message about petitionary prayer:

> Ask, and it will be given to you;
> search, and you will find;
> knock, and the door will be opened for you.
>> (Matthew 7:7)

Some aphorisms are deliberately riddling and meant to be puzzled over, such as:

> For to those who have, more will be given;
> and from those who have nothing, even what they have will be taken away.

> (Mark 4:25)

The major forms of Jesus' teaching are tailored for an oral society: parables for a storytelling culture, aphorisms for a culture that valued proverbs and maxims, riddles for a culture in which brain-teasers were good entertainment. Moreover, these sayings are carefully crafted. They are not extemporary speech but prepared formulations. Jesus would not have spoken them only once, but used them frequently in his teaching. Most are also mnemonic, that is, designed to be memorable. Jesus must have expected his disciples to remember them, as indeed they did. It is not unlikely, since rote learning was widely practised in the ancient world, that the disciples deliberately committed them to memory, though not necessarily in exact words. If Jesus taught the crowds and his disciples at length, as the Gospels relate, he must also have spoken more discursively, but in the parables and aphorisms we have the forms in which Jesus encapsulated his teaching. They are the sayings he designed to be remembered, and so they are what we have in the Synoptic Gospels. The writers of these Gospels have represented Jesus' sermons by compiling parables and aphorisms and have also placed them in typical settings. The Gospel of John has adopted a different strategy. It incorporates remembered sayings of Jesus, but places them, as Jesus would have done, within longer discourses in a different style. These more discursive sermons and dialogues the author has fashioned from his own reflection on the remembered sayings of Jesus, but they serve to represent the way Jesus would have taught when speaking at length.

Finally, we should notice the intensity with which Jesus seems to have devoted himself to teaching, which must partly explain why, in such a short period, he made such an impression. When travelling from place to place and wherever he was welcome, he preached in synagogues. He taught large crowds in the open country. When in Jerusalem, he taught in the Temple courts. When invited out to dinner, he made the conversation an opportunity to teach. He taught intensively his small group of chosen disciples, on the road or wherever they stayed. He taught women as well as men, not something one may take for granted in that society. He conversed with learned seekers, like Nicodemus, far into the night. He debated with other teachers, and took questions, sincere or hostile, with alacrity. The only social contexts he seems to have avoided were non-Jewish ones (we shall later consider why) and the Galilean cities of Sepphoris and Tiberius, perhaps because they were dangerous for a fugitive from the ire of Herod Antipas. But, most unusually for a Jewish teacher, he did preach to the people Jews thought of as only pseudo-Israelites: Samaritans.

Abba, the God of the kingdom

The wellspring of Jesus' life and activity was his relationship with the God he called 'Father'. He devoted himself to this God and to the mission he believed he had been given by him. This God, the God whose rule Jesus announced and enacted, was, without reservation, the God of the Hebrew Scriptures. He was the God who created all things and who exercised sovereign authority over all things. Further, he was the God who chose Israel to be his special people, required them to live lives devoted to him alone, and gave them his law, the Torah, to enable them to do so. He was a God of generosity, compassion, and reliability. The Hebrew Bible most often sums up his character in the phrase 'abounding in steadfast love and faithfulness', but reckons also with his awe-inspiring holiness. While his patience and forgiveness usually characterize the way he deals with the rebellion and wickedness of his people, they are not to be presumed on. While he characteristically takes the part of the poor and the weak, he unrelentingly condemns the persistently wicked.

Much of what the Jews knew of their God took the form of story. The Hebrew Bible tells a grand narrative of God's dealings with the world and with Israel. In Jesus' time, Jewish teachers were constantly retelling the story to bring out its relevance to their contemporary situation, while ordinary Jews were constantly reminded of the key elements of the story at the annual festivals in the Temple. It was a story with a future in which God would fulfil his many promises to Israel, and, furthermore, would realize his intention, through Israel, to become the one God of all the nations. Jesus' message of the arrival of the kingdom of God took up this story. God was beginning to re-establish and to complete his rule, beginning with his own people but with his whole creation in view. This God, whose kingdom Jesus announced, was the same God of Israel who had brought his people out of slavery in Egypt, given them his law, and settled them in their land. But it would not be surprising that there was also an element of novelty in the way that Jesus thought of God's relationship to his people now that God was doing what the prophets had called a new thing, something unheard of in the story so far. So in fact, we may observe that, while Jesus rejects nothing in the biblical portrayal or story of God, there is something of a new configuration of themes in his own representation of God. It seems that he even gives God a new name.

Among the Jews of Jesus' time, great importance was attached to the way one spoke of God, with special concern for reverence. God's special name, YHWH, the four letters or tetragrammaton God had revealed to Moses, was by Jesus' time never pronounced, except by the high priest once a year. A variety of reverential substitutes were used. Jesus himself, of course, never uses this name, but nor does he use the most common substitute 'Lord' (the substitute that most English versions of the Old Testament still employ). Of course, he uses the word 'God', but much less often than we might expect, and he frequently uses a Jewish way of speaking that avoids direct reference to God's action by using passive verbs. For example, when Jesus says, 'Blessed are those who mourn, for they will be comforted', he means: 'for God will comfort them'.

However, what makes Jesus' God-talk rather different from the practice of his Jewish contemporaries can be seen in the remarkable fact that, whereas Jesus speaks constantly of 'the kingdom of God', he never, in direct speech about God, refers to God as 'King'. Within the parables, the figure who stands for God is rarely a king, but commonly a householder, landowner, or father. Outside the parables, Jesus never calls God 'King' and very rarely 'Lord'. The one term that he does use with relative frequency is 'Father'. In the Jewish literature of the period, on the other hand, God was pervasively represented as King or Lord, but only rarely as Father. Now clearly Jesus was not rejecting or even downplaying God's sovereign authority. Otherwise the term 'kingdom of God' would not be so central in his teaching. But he seems to have been only too aware of the limitations of the analogy with human kings, given their generally oppressive rule. In God's case, the inner character of his rule was better described as fatherhood.

We should not forget that in the ancient world kings often claimed to be the fathers of their subjects, indicating their benevolent care for their people. Moreover, the everyday understanding of fatherhood in Jewish society and ideology included an essential element of responsible authority. (The fifth of the Ten Commandments required children to honour their parents.) In highlighting God's fatherhood, Jesus will have been very aware that the image combined authority and loving care. We can observe both in his actual use of the image. In itself, this was nothing new. In the Hebrew Bible and later Jewish literature, God is represented as the father of Israel his son, though relatively rarely. When the image is used, what it stresses is God's loving care and protection, his compassion and forgiveness, sometimes his loving correction of wayward children, and the expectation that children should honour and obey their father is sometimes explicit. Jesus was taking up a thoroughly Jewish way of thinking of God but privileging it over others.

A further remarkable fact is that, according to all four Gospels, when Jesus addressed God in prayer he always called God 'Father', with the single exception of his desolate cry from the cross, which was a quotation of a psalm ('My God, my God why have you forsaken me?'). Even here, the chosen words (the reduplicated 'my God') stress intimate personal relationship. Usually Jesus' address to God is 'Father' alone; only once do we find, 'Father, Lord of heaven and earth'. And it is clear that by 'Father', Jesus means 'my Father', not 'our Father'. He teaches his disciples to pray 'Father', meaning 'our Father', but never includes himself in such an 'our Father'. With this usage, we can compare the fact that in Jewish literature of the period much the most usual forms of address to God evoked his authority as Lord or King. In standard Jewish liturgical usage from a later date, God is regularly addressed as 'our Father', most often along with 'our King', and it is very likely that such usage goes back to the time of Jesus. For an individual to pray to God as 'my Father' is extremely rarely evidenced.

Finally, we must notice that the actual word Jesus used in his address to God was the Aramaic word 'Abba'. It is remarkable that Mark's Gospel, though written in Greek, preserves this word in Jesus' native tongue. This word was not, as has sometimes been thought, exclusively a small child's word, but it was the word that a son or daughter would ordinarily use, from childhood to adulthood, within the family context. While any use of 'my Father' or 'our Father' would evoke the intimacy of family relationships, Jesus' choice of Abba accentuates that fact. We have no other evidence of its use in prayer to God, though this does not, of course, prove that Jesus' usage was unique. It does, however, suggest at least relative distinctiveness and a deliberate choice of this term on Jesus' part. It is also significant, as we know from Paul's letters, that this actual Aramaic word continued to be used, not only by Aramaic-speaking Christians, but even by

Greek-speaking Christians in contexts where Aramaic was
unknown. The early Christians must have thought this a special
word, with which Jesus expressed his own relationship with God,
but which he also taught his disciples to use. Some words of Jesus
help to explain this:

> All things have been handed over to me by my Father;
> and no one knows the son except the father,
> and no one knows the father except the son
> and anyone to whom the son chooses to reveal him.
>
> (Matthew 11:27)

Here Jesus speaks of the unparalleled intimacy between a father
and his son, as though this was his own special privilege, but he
also envisages a sharing of this privileged access to the father with
others. This is a family into which others can be introduced.

We should probably suppose that Jesus' own profound experience
of God was as a loving intimacy that required his devotion and
obedience to God. He chose the word 'Abba' to express this – in
the first place to himself and to God. But he also understood his
mission from his Father to be the enactment of God's kingdom,
which meant a renewal of God's people Israel and their
relationship with God. This was happening as the activity of God's
compassionate and forgiving love. It was something both old and
new. It was the love of the God Israel had always known to be
their father. But it was also the new thing, the new covenant
relationship that the prophets had foreseen. When Jesus spoke of
God as Abba and taught his disciples to use that word, he must
have seen the compassionate love of God that he knew in his own
experience overflowing to others.

Perhaps we should think of Abba as a new *name* of God. At the
origins of God's people Israel, at the time of their Exodus from
Egypt, God gave Moses the name YHWH as the name by which
his people were to address him. He was not an unknown God. He

had already been known as the God of Abraham, Isaac, and Jacob. But a new chapter of his story with his people was beginning, and the name YHWH corresponded with that. Similarly, Jesus may have understood Abba to be the new name of God that corresponded to the new beginning, the new exodus, the new covenant with his people that God was initiating. It was the name by which the renewed Israel would know him, not, of course, superseding YHWH, but added, as though it were the new substitute for the name that could not be said.

The prayer that Jesus gave to his disciples begins: 'Father, may your name be sanctified'. This version in Luke's Gospel surely reflects the original Aramaic Abba, whereas the better-known version in Matthew's Gospel ('Our Father in heaven, may your name be sanctified') is more of a paraphrase. Though a Jewish audience would naturally take the name to be YHWH, maybe Jesus meant it to be Abba. This would explain why this particular Aramaic word was so important to the early Christians that even Greek speakers went on using it. 'Father, may your name be sanctified' combines that Jewish reverence for the holy name of God that Jesus clearly shared, with the overwhelming sense of God's intimate and compassionate love that drove Jesus' special mission from his Abba.

In the modern period, Jesus' teaching about the fatherhood of God has been much misunderstood. Jesus did not mean that all people are children of God by virtue of their creation by God. This idea is not to be found in the Hebrew Bible, in early Jewish literature, or in the New Testament. Throughout these bodies of literature, fatherhood refers to God's relationship of intimacy with his covenant people. Nor is Jesus' understanding of God's fatherhood a 'new idea' of God. What divine fatherhood meant for Jesus is all to be found in the Hebrew Bible (with the exception perhaps of Jesus' sense of his own uniquely privileged intimacy with his Abba). What was new was what God was doing.

Finally, it is a modern mistake to imagine that the love of God as Jesus portrays it excludes God's righteous anger. This God of generosity and forgiveness condemns severely those who spurn his generosity, reject his forgiveness, and continue on the destructive path of evil. Jesus' preaching of the kingdom is full of the urgency of the need for decision lest judgement follow.

Interpreting Torah

In Jewish tradition, there were two ways in which teachers gave instruction in how to live. The first was interpretation of the law of Moses, focusing on definition of what precisely each commandment required. The second was wisdom instruction: wise counsel on how to live, provided by a sage, often encapsulated in carefully composed aphorisms. The book of Proverbs is the classic example of wisdom instruction within the Hebrew Scriptures. In the time of Jesus, these two traditions were by no means entirely separate. The law itself was understood to embody divine wisdom, and wisdom instruction was rooted in the law. But still the two types of teaching are relatively distinct.

Most of Jesus' teaching is in the style of wisdom instruction, and he only occasionally engaged in the sort of legal discussion that occupied the Pharisees and the Essenes. But this does not mean that he did not interpret Torah. For Jesus, as for all Jewish teachers, the Torah was the instructions God had given his people for them to live by. At a time when various Jewish groups distinguished themselves largely by their particular ways of interpreting Torah, Jesus must be expected to do the same and to find himself in debate with other Jewish teachers. What we find is that Jesus had a very distinctive approach to interpreting Torah. He did not, as some modern interpreters of Jesus have supposed, rescind the Torah or deliberately flout it, but in some cases his interpretation was so radical it is not surprising it has been seen in that way. He certainly did not identify with any of the available traditions of interpretation. The authoritative traditions of the Pharisees he swept scornfully aside, and went his own innovating way.

Jesus was once asked by a legal expert which of the commandments of the Torah he considered the most important. The question was probably not unusual. The 613 commandments range from very broad moral requirements to very specific rules of many kinds. Any attempt to live by these commandments requires some judgements about priorities, and certainly Jewish teachers of a later date are known to have offered opinions on which laws are the most important, without, of course, implying that others could be ignored. Perhaps Jesus' answer was not original, but it is certainly distinctive. In Mark's version it is:

> The first [commandment] is, 'Hear, O Israel: the Lord our God, the Lord is one; you shall love the Lord your God with all your heart, and with all your soul, and with all your mind, and with all your strength.' The second is this, 'You shall love your neighbour as yourself.' There is no other commandment greater than these.
>
> (Mark 12:30,31)

Though asked only to name the one most important commandment, Jesus volunteers two. Modern readers do not always appreciate that both these commandments are quoted from the Mosaic law. Jesus did not invent an ethic of love, but singled out as the most important two commandments with which his interlocutor and any bystanders would have been very familiar. The first, known as the *Shema*, was recited daily by all devout Jews. It was the nearest thing to a Jewish creed. The Torah itself, however, does not bring it into connection with the command to love the neighbour. Within the Torah, these two commandments are widely separated. But in bringing them together, Jesus employed a standard Jewish technique of scriptural study, which involved relating passages containing the same words. These are two of only four passages in the Torah in which the precise grammatical phrase, 'You shall love...' occurs.

The demand for complete devotion to the one and only God takes priority. We see once again how focused Jesus was on God. He was very far from the modern habit of collapsing love of God into love of neighbour. Love of God does, however, require love of neighbour. It is also obvious that love is not primarily emotional. As an obedient response to a divine commandment, it is a matter of will and action, though the *Shema* also makes it clear that it must involve the whole of one's inner being. Obedience from the heart is required, and we shall see that this emphasis on inner motivation is typical of Jesus.

What is the effect of the prioritizing of these two commandments on interpretation of the rest of the law? One possibility is that these commandments should override others in cases of conflict between laws. Such conflict is normal in codes of laws, and Jewish teachers recognized that. For example, the Torah requires that one circumcise a male child on the eighth day after birth. But suppose this day is a Sabbath, the day on which all work is prohibited. One of these two commandments must take precedence over the other. That Jesus intended his prioritizing of the command to love the neighbour to override other laws can be seen in the well-known parable of the Good Samaritan, though modern readers unfamiliar with the detailed requirements of Torah do not easily recognize this.

In the parable, a man who has been attacked by robbers lies half-dead at the side of the road. The first two passers-by are a priest and a levite (Temple assistant). They carefully keep their distance from the dying man. The Torah specifically forbids priests to contract corpse impurity by coming close to a corpse, unless the dead person is a close relative. Levites are likely to have been expected to maintain the same standard of ritual purity as the priests. There was no such requirement for lay Israelites, which explains why Jesus has made these two characters in the story a priest and a levite. They cannot tell whether the man is actually dead without coming so close that, if he were dead, they would contract corpse impurity. In effect, they allow the law forbidding them to contract corpse impurity to override the commandment to love their neighbour, which obviously requires them to help the man, if he is still alive.

The parable invites its hearers to judge the priest and the levite wrong and to approve, probably against their natural inclinations, of the Samaritan–one of the apostate nation who observed the law of Moses, but, in Jewish eyes, inadequately. The Samaritan, who would not be expected to understand Torah correctly, is the one who understands how the love of neighbour must overrule all other considerations, such as the bitter religious feud between Jews and Samaritans. The parable works by initially arousing its hearers' sympathy for the dying man and thereby nudging them in the direction of recognizing the overriding importance of the duty to love the neighbour. The fact that the hero of the story turns out to be a Samaritan shocks them into realizing that there are no circumstances in which someone desperately in need of help does not constitute the neighbour they are obliged to love. Jesus does not here reject the rules for priestly purity, but he downgrades them. Weightier considerations take precedence.

In the Hebrew Bible, the 'neighbour' one was commanded to love was one's fellow Israelite. But Jesus treated the command in the same way as he treated a number of other key moral demands of the law. He extended its implications as far as possible. With Jesus' command to 'love enemies', he removed any limit on the commandment, as though one had to love fellow Israelites but was permitted to hate other people. Although the principle of non-retaliation, not returning evil for evil, can be found occasionally before Jesus, he does seem to have been original in formulating a commandment to 'love enemies', meaning positively to do good to those who hate one. Particularly striking is the fact that, since personal enemies within Jewish society were already included in the 'neighbours' one should love, the enemies whom

Jesus insists one should love must be national enemies. Romans would be in every hearer's thoughts.

A similar process of extending by removing limits explains some cases where Jesus' interpretation might seem to be a straightforward contradiction of a Mosaic command. In contrast to the command not to lie on oath, Jesus tells his disciples not to use oaths at all. (The issue is not 'swearing' in the modern colloquial sense, but the more serious business of swearing an oath in order to guarantee one's truthfulness.) Jesus here is demanding total truthfulness. The Torah required truthfulness at least when one spoke on oath, but if Jesus' disciples are truthful at all times, they should not need to use oaths. Another case is the principle of just retribution in the law: 'an eye for an eye and a tooth for a tooth'. The purpose of the law was to limit retaliation to just proportions. Jesus asks his disciples to go one better: do not retaliate at all.

In other cases, Jesus extends a command by interiorization. Not only should one not murder; one should not harbour the anger that may lead to murder. Not only should one not commit adultery; one should not nourish the lust that may lead to adultery. This kind of penetration to the springs of motivation is not at all alien to the law. The last commandment of the Decalogue itself, the command not to covet, reaches into the thoughts of the heart. Jesus gives the commands not to murder or to commit adultery the same kind of inner reference.

All these are examples of a broad pattern of extending or intensifying the law. We could see it as a programme for greater holiness for the people of God that both compares and contrasts with the programme of the Pharisees. The Pharisees too were engaged in intensifying the law, but their focus was on ritual purity, aiming at a higher level of purity than the letter of the law required, and on scrupulous observance of such matters as tithing and Sabbath. In his polemical attacks on them, Jesus can accuse them of attending to these while neglecting the weightier matters, the moral demands of the law. In one of his more sarcastic jibes, Jesus said that they 'strain out a gnat' (removing a tiny source of impurity from their drink) 'but swallow a camel' (the largest animal in Palestine). We need not suppose that the moral virtues did not concern the Pharisees, but their concentration on increased ritual purity, contrasted with Jesus' downgrading of ritual purity in favour of intensified moral demands, explains why they often clashed. Both deeply concerned with the holiness of the people of God, they approached it in very different ways.

It seems that conflict between Jesus and Pharisaic teachers focused especially on the observation of the Sabbath. Even more than food laws and purity rules, observing the Sabbath was a mark of Jewish identity, defining them over against non-Jews as the holy people of God. This may account for the special degree of hostility to Jesus aroused by his alleged violations of the Sabbath, which consisted of healing people without life-threatening conditions, as well as an occasion when his disciples plucked grains of wheat to assuage their hunger. It is important to notice that Jewish groups in the time of Jesus in any case differed over the degree of rigour with which the prohibition of work on the Sabbath was interpreted. Essenes took a more rigorous line than Pharisees. Jesus was taking a position of his own within a current debate. Also significant is the idea that sometimes a more important principle might override a less important law (noticed above in connection with the parable of the Good Samaritan). A version of this approach was widely held in relation to the Sabbath, where it was accepted that one might break the Sabbath in order to save one's own or another life. Saving the life of a domestic animal could also be justified. Jesus extended the application of this kind of consideration to situations that were not life-threatening: healing of serious, but not fatal, conditions, and assuaging hunger in a situation where his disciples could perhaps not have obtained food easily without doing the 'work' of plucking grain, but were not actually starving. A broader principle that Jesus enunciates is that the Sabbath was meant as a gift, not a burden ('The Sabbath was made for humanity, not humanity of the Sabbath').

The Sabbath controversies are revealing in several ways. First, Jesus here rather clearly engages with an issue that was already in debate between Jewish teachers, though he does not seem to have been interested in joining in the debate until his practice was challenged. Second, while Jesus considerably extends the category of work permitted on the Sabbath beyond the limits set by others, he does not lay down a clearly defined limit of his own. He leaves the category somewhat open-ended. He is concerned with the sorts of things that are appropriate on the Sabbath but not with determining precisely what is and is not permitted, as the Pharisees were in this and many other issues of legal interpretation. Thirdly, in the case of plucking grain, Jesus advances some scriptural arguments, but resorts in the end to asserting his own authority: 'The Son of man is lord of the Sabbath'.

By no means everything in Jesus' interpretation of Torah is original or distinctive, especially when we remember that such matters were in debate between the various Jewish groups. But it is also apparent that Jesus exercises far more freedom in how he interprets the commandments than others were accustomed to doing. He identifies the spirit of the Torah and develops it in ways that go far beyond the letter of the commandments. He seriously downgrades the importance of aspects of Torah that many of his contemporaries emphasized. Moreover, he does not so much argue as pronounce authoritatively on the meaning of the commandments. At the end of the Sermon on the Mount, where much of Jesus' interpretation of Torah is collected, Matthew's Gospel comments that 'the crowds were astounded at his teaching, for he taught them as one having authority, and not as their scribes'. The scribes here are the legal experts. Jesus does not rely on knowledge of the tradition or professional expertise, but speaks as someone comparable, one might suppose, with Moses himself, who knew the will of God at firsthand.

Jesus' interpretation of Torah cannot, of course, be unrelated to his distinctive message of the arrival of the kingdom of God. For this reason, though it competed with the Pharisaic programme of holiness for the nation, it was also distinctive in being an interpretation of Torah for a new situation. It was for those who recognized that the rule of God was at hand and committed themselves to live out the will of God as that situation demanded. This is not to say that Jesus interpreted the Torah for the age to come when God's kingdom will have been perfected on earth. Jesus' teaching presumes an ordinary world in which Israel has enemies, people get mugged by thieves, and marriage still happens. But it must be intended for those who seek to live already, in present circumstances, under the coming rule of God. This means that the intensity or the extremity of Jesus' reading of Torah is not merely pedagogic, though it does serve to press home the need to take the commandments with absolute seriousness. It must also relate to the new possibilities of life that are opened up by the closeness of the kingdom. Although there is no textual allusion to support this point, it seems likely that Jesus was influenced by the prophet Jeremiah's prophecy of the new covenant. In this God promised, 'I will put my law within them, and I will write it on their hearts'. At any rate, this coheres very well with Jesus' emphasis on the integrity of the heart as the source of all true obedience to the law.

A different society

We have already noted Jesus' concern to contrast the rule of God with earthly rule, which appears in his privileging of the image of God as Father over the image of God as King. The contrast is developed in more concrete ways when Jesus speaks of the kinds of social relationships that are to characterize the community of his disciples, the kinds of relationships that prevail when God's rule is actualized in a society of people devoted to it. In a series of highly distinctive rejections of current social structures and relationships, Jesus portrays a society in which none of the claims to rank and status that were taken for granted in his world has any place at all.

Jesus sometimes characterizes his community as the family of those who know God as Jesus' Father and as their own Father. On an occasion when Jesus was with a group of his disciples, he was told that his mother and siblings were at the door, asking for him. Evidently they thought that his activities were getting out of hand and had come to persuade him to go back home to Nazareth with them. The apparent harshness of Jesus' reply stems from his absolute commitment to his mission from God. 'Who are my mother and my brothers?' he said, and, looking around him, added: 'Here are my mother and my brothers! Whoever does the will of God is my brother and sister and mother' (Mark 3:31–33). Jesus, who does his Father's will, constitutes those who join him in this a family related to God as their Father. Consequently, there are no human fathers in this community. Elsewhere, in the same vein, Jesus speaks of disciples who have left mothers, fathers, siblings, and children for the sake of the kingdom. In the kingdom, they are compensated by finding their fellow disciples to be mothers, siblings, and children – but fathers are not listed. The patriarchal status, with its distinctive authority, is reserved for God. Instead of the fatherhood of God being the paradigm of patriarchal privilege, it excludes it.

Jesus' most socially radical statements concern slaves, children, and the poor. He made a sharp contrast between the oppressive regimes of the Gentiles (he did not have to instance Rome in particular) and the way things should happen in God's kingdom. In the latter, he said, 'whoever wishes to become great among you must be your servant, and whoever wishes to be first among you must be slave of all' (Mark 10:42–45). Jesus endorsed this statement with his own, shocking example, when he insisted, against their protests, on washing his disciples' feet. Washing feet, an everyday menial task, was, more exclusively than any other task, the role of the slave. It was what every free person regarded as unthinkably beneath their dignity. Jesus enjoined his disciples to follow his example by washing one another's feet, and he was proposing, not a mere symbol of humility, but an actual concrete instance, the most telling possible, of how the disciples should relate to each other. The ordinary everyday requirement of washing feet they are to do for each other. If this is not beneath their dignity, nothing is.

Jesus thus took the unparalleled step of abolishing social status, not by giving all the disciples the status of master (then there would always be others, outside the community, to set themselves above), but by reducing all to the lowest social status: that of slave. In a society of slaves, no one may think him- or herself more important than others.

Also strikingly original is Jesus' choice of small children to illustrate what God's rule requires. Only by becoming like a child is it possible to enter the kingdom. The point is probably not so much the unquestioning trust that children display, but the fact that they had no social status. To become like a child is to renounce any claim to status above others. Just as Jesus said that the one who wants to be foremost must be the slave of all, so he also says that 'whoever becomes humble like this child is the greatest in the kingdom', where 'humble' is an attitude relating to social status. At first sight, it looks as though Jesus was creating a new form of hierarchy, a sort of inverted one, in which the most slave-like or the most childlike is top, but really these sayings serve to subvert all notions of status or rank. The same is true of his aphorism: 'Many who are first will be last, and the last will be first.' The kingdom is a topsy-turvy world that inverts all claims to personal importance in order to do away with all self-importance.

The kingdom belongs to the likes of children, just as it also belongs to the likes of the poor. This is the essence of what it means that Jesus preaches 'good news to the poor': he tells them that the kingdom of God belongs to them. These poor, as we have noticed, are not the ordinary people, but the destitute, the people at the bottom of the social and economic heap. Jesus does not suppose that the kingdom belongs exclusively to them, but that they are the model citizens to which everyone else must conform. The least radical implication is the advice Jesus gives to ordinarily prosperous people, when they give dinner parties, not to invite their relatives, friends, and neighbours, but 'the poor, the crippled, the lame and the blind'. This is more than generous charity, which was a well-recognized duty. It means treating the destitute as one's social equals. On these terms, but only on these terms, Jesus did not confine the kingdom to the destitute, any more than he confined it to the children. He did very seriously privilege the destitute and the children, in order to deprive all others of privilege.

The poor require a little more attention. We have the series of 'beatitudes', with which Jesus characterized the model citizens of the kingdom, in two versions. In Luke's version, the first beatitude is 'Blessed are you who are poor, for yours is the kingdom of God'. In Matthew's version, it is 'Blessed are the poor in spirit, for theirs is the kingdom of heaven'. Matthew's expansion of 'the poor' to 'the poor in spirit' does not imply that he removes the socio-economic meaning, transforming poverty into simply an attitude. Rather, in the background, is the Jewish tradition of linking poverty with the right attitude to God, just as wealth was linked with the wrong attitude to God. The poor, having nowhere else to turn, are aware of their utter dependence on God, whereas the rich, feeling self-sufficient, epitomize arrogant independence of God. These are, of course, stereotypes, but, at least in a society that took a religious worldview for granted, not without correspondence to reality. Matthew's phrase 'poor in spirit' merely makes explicit the link between material circumstances and religious attitude that is implicit in Luke's simple 'poor'.

Thus the poor model citizenship in God's kingdom not only in their lack of socio-economic status and resources but also in the kind of relationship with God that typified that status. Jesus, we are reminded again, never thinks of relationships between humans without reference to God. What transforms society in Jesus' ideal is knowing God as the utterly reliable and endlessly generous provider of all good, on whom all creatures are completely dependent. Trusting this God is what enables the generous sharing among people that makes God's generosity credible. The kind of trust in God's provision that Jesus envisaged is enshrined in one petition of the Lord's prayer: 'Give us this day our daily bread'. Adequate provision for material needs, not luxury, and day-by-day provision, not wealth stored up, are all that is asked. It puts every disciple of Jesus in the position of the beggars, who depend day-by-day on charity, or the day labourers, those agricultural workers who had least security, employed only a day at a time, never earning more than the next day's meal requires. Jesus requires of all disciples the radical trust that for the destitute is the only sort available.

The Temple theocracy and the Roman Empire

What then of Jesus' position on the Jewish political issues of the day? If he can be said to have addressed them, it was not directly but with the indirectness characteristic of his teaching style. His primary concern was with the nature of God's rule over his own people. From Jesus' perspective, the Jewish theocracy, that is, the chief priests who ran the Temple and claimed to represent God's rule over his people, grossly misrepresented the nature of God's rule. Instead of differing from the way the kings of the Gentiles ruled, they imitated it. Jesus' act of protest in the Temple, when he attacked the money-changers and the people selling animals for sacrifice, is of key significance here. Because the chief priests were running the Temple and the sacrificial system as a profit-making business, they hindered access to God's gracious presence in his house, especially for the poor.

8. Model of 1st-century Jerusalem with the Temple in the foreground

Some of the Jewish revolutionaries might have agreed with Jesus on this point, but he differed from them in at least two respects. In the first place, violent revolution would be hard to square with Jesus' requirement to love enemies. But, secondly, this difference was really just part of Jesus' overall concern for a radically different kind of society, a concern that demoted the issue of independence from Rome to a secondary matter at best. Jesus' vision of God's rule was not of a Jewish state liberated from Roman rule, but of a society formed by the experience of God's healing and forgiving grace, sustained by God's fatherly provision, inclusive of all those who tend to be left out of or pushed to the margins of society, characterized not by domination but by mutual service, and in which all status and privilege are replaced by brotherly, sisterly, and motherly relationships of loving mutuality. This is not at all to say that it was 'non-political': like most Jewish religion and most ancient politics, it was religio-political. But it differed from the most popular Jewish political options of the time.

The warning of destruction

The parable of Jesus commonly known as the 'Unmerciful Servant' is set, unusually, at the court of a fabulously wealthy ruler. The unusual setting, far from the ordinary experience of Jesus' hearers, is needed so that the king can be portrayed as extraordinarily generous. The slaves of the king, who are the other characters in the story, are his high-ranking government officials, themselves very powerful and wealthy men, though wholly subject to the will of the king. One of these men owes the king the sort of sum of money we now call astronomical, way beyond the imagination of anyone in Jesus' audience. When the king orders him to repay the debt, it transpires, not surprisingly, that he cannot do so. He pleads for mercy. What he asks is time to repay. It does not occur to him to ask to be forgiven the debt, so unthinkable would such a notion be. But this is precisely what the king does. He simply writes off the debt. This is the moment, so frequent in parables, of surprise. But what follows is equally surprising. One would expect the king's act of extravagant generosity to make a difference to the slave's subsequent behaviour, but it does not. Just as he is leaving the king's presence, the slave comes upon one of his fellow slaves, who, it so happens, owes him money, though the sum is a tiny fraction of the debt the king has forgiven. The scene before the king is repeated. The slave demands repayment, the fellow slave begs to be given time to pay. But instead of imitating the king's generosity, the slave has the man put in the debtors' prison until he can pay. When the king hears of it, he is naturally furious, revokes his mercy, and sends the slave to be punished until he repays the entire debt. We can hardly imagine he will ever be able to do so (Matthew 18:23–34).

The two surprises in the parable are the astonishing generosity of the king and the astonishing failure of the slave to let it make any difference to his behaviour. But within the world of the parable, it is not surprising that the king then retracts his mercy.

In effect, he is saying to the slave, 'Have it your own way!' His extravagant generosity should have transformed the slave's world, but the slave chooses to remain in a world where mercy is unknown. It is really he himself who has refused truly to accept the king's mercy, holding it at arm's length while getting on with business as usual.

The parable elaborates an image Jesus uses elsewhere, not least within the Lord's Prayer, where (in Matthew's version) we find the same use of debt as an image of sin and the same connection between being forgiven and forgiving: 'Forgive us our debts, as we also have forgiven our debtors'. But what especially concerns us now is the way Jesus can hold together the extravagant generosity of God and the same God's unmitigated condemnation of those who reject it. It is a combination many modern readers find hard to understand, but it is typical of Jesus' teaching.

The dark side of Jesus' teaching – the warning of destruction – follows from the seriousness with which he takes the mercy and compassion of God that his message makes available. It is the critical moment in Israel's history. The kingdom is within reach. To know that and to refuse this extravagant generosity of God is to exclude oneself from the kingdom. The judgement is really self-imposed. Jesus could hardly suppose that there could be any way of achieving some kind of human fulfilment outside the kingdom of God. The kingdom is the consummate good that God has provided for all his people. So those who see the door to the kingdom wide open to them but choose not to enter forfeit the one and only human destiny.

When Jesus spoke of divine judgement to come, he was issuing a warning. He gave the warning so that judgement might be avoided, and when he contemplated the consequences of his message being rejected, it was evidently with great sadness, as appears in his tender lament over the city of Jerusalem:

> How often have I desired to gather your children together as a hen
> gathers her brood under her wings, but you were not willing! See,
> your house is left to you, desolate.
>
> (Matthew 23:37–38)

Here, Jesus speaks of the fate of the city ('your house' is perhaps the Temple), but on some occasions, he is clearly considering the final fate of individuals. Jesus does not appear to have had a conceptually systematic view of the future, but deployed a number of images. There is, for example, the image of the great banquet from which people might find themselves excluded. There is the judicial image of the courtroom where all people will be called to account and face the judgement of God. There are analogies from scriptural history: the great Flood and the destruction of Sodom and Gomorrah, both judgements that some escaped.

Chapter 6
A question of identity

Clearly, Jesus claimed a special relationship with God and a special mission from God. After his death, the Jewish followers of Jesus proclaimed that he was the Messiah of Israel promised in the Hebrew Bible. But this was actually the least they claimed for him, for they went on to associate him with God in ways that went beyond what was expected of any human Messiah. How far was any of this anticipated before Jesus' death?

Authority

What seems most to have impressed people about Jesus in his lifetime is the 'authority' with which he spoke and acted. The Greek word indicates the power to command and to effect one's commands. About his teaching, people said that he taught with authority, unlike the scribes, the legal experts who relied on professional expertise to do no more than apply traditional teaching. When he claimed the authority to forgive sins, the scribes were shocked because only God had the authority to forgive sins. His exorcisms were recognized as the exercise of authority over the powers of evil. The only way the scribes could explain this was to accuse Jesus of collusion with those powers.

In the case of forgiving sins, what was at issue was not, of course, the ability of an individual to forgive someone for the wrong done to that individual. Rather, the issue concerned God's prerogative of forgiving sin committed against himself, as ultimately all sin is. When Jesus said, 'Your sins are forgiven', he would no doubt be understood to be using a 'divine passive', meaning, 'God forgives your sins'. But this is not a prayer for God to forgive. It is an unequivocal declaration of God's forgiveness, as though Jesus claims the right to speak for God. Indeed, he explains that 'the Son of man [Jesus] has authority on earth to forgive sins' (Mark 2:5,10). In the whole of early Jewish literature, there seems to be only one other case in which God's forgiveness is declared by a human being. It is in a story about the Babylonian king Nabonidus, who narrates how he was seriously ill, prayed to God, and a Jewish exorcist 'forgave my sin'. We do not know exactly what this meant (even the translation is not certain), but it remains the case that Jesus' practice of declaring God's forgiveness was perceived in his time as infringing a divine prerogative.

In the case of Jesus' exorcisms, it is remarkable that Jesus uses no techniques or incantations, utters no prayer to God, and invokes no name of a powerful being beyond himself. He does not tell demons to depart 'in the name of God', whereas his disciples do so 'in the name of Jesus', and we even hear of one case where a Jewish exorcist who was not among Jesus' disciples used the name of Jesus in order to expel demons by its power. Jesus seems simply to exercise God's authority over demons.

It may seem curious that Jesus avoids any direct explanation of the source of his authority. When he took it upon himself to clear the money-changers out of the Temple court, the Temple authorities asked by what authority he did so. Jesus evaded answering by putting to them a counter-question about the source of John the Baptist's authority, a question he knows they will not find it politic to answer. This is of a piece with his general reticence about his own role in the coming of the kingdom, to which we shall return.

It could be said, however, that Jesus indicates the source of his authority in the characteristically indirect form of a parable. In the Parable of the Vineyard, the vineyard is a familiar image of Israel, while the tenants presumably represent the Jewish leadership, and the absentee landlord represents God. The owner sends one slave after another to collect his share of the produce from the tenants, but in every case, they beat or even kill the slave. Eventually, the owner sends his 'beloved son', supposing that they surely must respect the special authority of a son to represent his father. In fact, the tenants kill him too.

This parable connects with the indications we have already noticed that Jesus understood himself to be in a uniquely special relationship to Abba, his divine Father. Just as the son in the parable transcends the role of the slaves, so Jesus spoke and acted with God's authority in a way that went beyond how prophets and other figures in the Jewish tradition usually did.

Messiah?

In view of the way Jesus was seen to exercise authority, it is not surprising that people saw him as a prophet. Many identified him, more precisely, as *the* prophet, the prophet who was expected to come at the climax of Israel's history to restore the state God intended for them. This prophet was often envisaged as a prophet like Moses, who would lead Israel in a new exodus. Jesus fitted this bill rather well. Like Moses, he taught with authority, and, like Moses, he performed miraculous 'deeds of power', though mostly of a rather different kind. When Jesus did perform a miracle closely resembling one of Moses' miracles, providing food for a crowd of people in the wilderness, they understandably thought he must surely be the expected prophet like Moses, and attempted to make him king. (Moses, as a leader of the people, was sometimes identified as a king as well as a prophet.) Jesus declined the role.

The other role into which many of Jesus' contemporaries wished to fit him was that of the royal Messiah of David, the ideal king descended from King David. This figure was also popularly conceived as a leader who would liberate Israel from the Roman yoke, probably by armed force with divine assistance. But it is not so easy to understand why people identified Jesus as the royal Messiah as it is to understand why they thought he was the prophet like Moses. The expected son of David was not normally thought to be a teacher or a healer. Perhaps it was the strong impression of Jesus' power to defeat evil that people gained from his exorcisms that accounts for this. Most likely, it was Jesus' constant talk of the kingdom of God and its proximity that particularly encouraged the idea that he himself must be the human king through whom God would establish his kingdom. Despite the ways in which Jesus clearly did not fit the popular expectation of such a figure, such was the strength of the hope for a militant saviour that wishful thinking is likely to have focused on Jesus nonetheless, given that he seemed to be a figure with an important mission from God.

Jesus' own attitude to the title Messiah was very cautious. In none of the four Gospels does Jesus ever use the title Messiah of himself (except in two places where the word is clearly an interpretative gloss by the Gospel writer). Yet when Peter and the twelve said that they thought he was the Messiah, Jesus did not deny it. Instead, he told them to keep quiet about it, and went on to explain how he saw his destiny in terms of rejection and death. At Jesus' trial before the high priest, the high priest finally asked him directly whether he was the Messiah. According to Mark's Gospel, Jesus' reply was a straightforward 'I am', though Jesus goes on to say something that presumably makes a point about how he saw the role of Messiah. But in Matthew's and Luke's Gospels, Jesus' reply is 'You say that I am', which is not a repudiation of the title but more like an oblique way of accepting it. The obliqueness may be due to a reluctance by Jesus to make the claim for himself or it may reflect a sense of mismatch between what the high priest is likely to think about the Messiah and the way Jesus himself conceives the role.

What accounts for this rather equivocal attitude by Jesus to the term 'Messiah'? Probably Jesus was concerned that the term would raise the wrong expectations in a context where the most popular model of the Messiah was the military conqueror of Israel's enemies. This makes sense of the occasions when Jesus seems to have preferred his activities to speak for him, rather than claim a specific title for himself. Rather than answering directly John the Baptist's question whether he was 'the one who is to come', Jesus asked the disciples of John the Baptist to observe his healings and exorcisms. His most explicit public claim to messianic identity was, as we shall see, an enactment of messianic prophecy, but again with no verbal claim to the title.

We should remember that the Hebrew Bible contains a range of texts that might be understood to refer to the Messiah, and what sort of Messiah one envisaged depended a lot on which texts one emphasized. We can begin to see how Jesus found his role in Scripture by considering how, on his last visit to Jerusalem, only days before his death, he rode into Jerusalem on a donkey. He must have been deliberately enacting the prophecy of Zechariah, which addressed Jerusalem:

> Lo, your king comes to you;
> Triumphant and victorious is he,
> Humble and riding on a donkey.
> (Zechariah 9:9)

That on this occasion Jesus was at last coming out as Messiah is clear from his reception by the crowds, who hailed him as such. But the prophecy chosen, not a popular messianic text, represents the Messiah as the king who comes in peace and humility, not as a warrior (who would ride a horse). In the next chapter, we shall consider how Jesus' expectation of rejection and death was based in an unusual reading of the prophetic Scriptures, again providing a messianic role decisively different from the popular one.

Jesus' reply to the high priest highlights another, very different way in which Jesus' understanding of his messiahship was distinctive. He said: 'You will see the Son of man seated at the right hand of the Power and coming with the clouds of heaven' (Mark 14:62). The words are virtually all drawn from Scripture, but conflate two texts: from Psalm 110:1, where the king is seated at God's right hand, and from the prophet Daniel, where a figure 'like a son of man' comes with the clouds to receive the kingdom from God (Daniel 7:13). Both texts could easily be read as references to the messianic son of David, but Jesus' combination of them makes a specific point. He claims a position of authority, seated on God's right hand on the heavenly throne of the universe, which identifies him with God's own sovereignty over the world more closely than the usual image of a human Messiah ruling on earth. This is why the reaction of the high priest and his council is to declare Jesus guilty of blasphemy. It would not have been blasphemy simply to claim to be the Messiah, but they took Jesus to be claiming something more, something that sounded to them like an infringement of God's sole prerogative of universal sovereignty.

Other indications of Jesus' authority

We have seen that in a variety of well-attested ways, Jesus spoke and acted with an assumption of divine authority. Without explaining it, Jesus assumes that whatever he says or does carries the authority of God. Once we recognize this in some cases, we shall easily find it in others. For example, when Jesus selected the twelve disciples to represent the twelve tribes of Israel, he was following the precedent of the twelve princes of the tribes in the period of the Exodus. But in that story, it was not Moses but God who selected the princes. We have already noticed how Jesus required of his disciples a loyalty to him that took precedence even over responsibilities to parents and children.

Jesus spoke and acted as though he himself embodied the rule of God that he preached and enacted. So unprecedented and epoch-making was the arrival of God's kingdom in Jesus' activity, Jesus could speak as though people's eternal destiny depended on their response to this activity and therefore to Jesus himself:

> Everyone who acknowledges me before others,
> the Son of man will also acknowledge before the angels of God;
> but whoever denies me before others,
> will be denied before the angels of God.

> (Luke 12:8–9)

Jesus speaks here of the Last Judgement, claiming that people's response to him will be the criterion of their judgement but at the same time acknowledging the enormity of that claim by the indirect language he uses. Perhaps what made Jesus reticent about making such claims for himself in a completely unambiguous way was a sense that the extraordinary authority he exercised was given to him by God. As in the Parable of the Vineyard, it was the plenary authority of a father exercised by his son.

The identity of Jesus in the Gospel of John

A major difference between the Synoptic Gospels and the Gospel of John is that, whereas in the Synoptics Jesus is notably reticent about his identity, in John he frequently speaks explicitly about who he is and his relationship with God. Scholars have often explained this by saying that John has simply projected back onto Jesus the way that the early Christians thought about him. But this cannot be true. For example, whereas the earliest Christians constantly spoke of Jesus as the Messiah (Christ),

Jesus in John's Gospel abstains from calling himself Messiah, just as he does in the other Gospels. Although John explains that the purpose of his Gospel is to enable people to believe that Jesus is the Messiah, he does not put that belief onto Jesus' own lips. Conversely, whereas early Christians never called Jesus 'the Son of man', Jesus in John's Gospel uses that phrase as an enigmatic form of self-reference, just as he does in the other Gospels. In John's Gospel Jesus frequently speaks of himself as 'the Son' (along with calling God 'the Father'), but this usage is not absent from the other Gospels. It occurs in them in rare, but significant, examples. This gives the clue to what John is really doing. He is reflecting on Jesus' indirect claims and making explicit the full significance he finds in them. This is a retrospective perspective, but it does not consist in attributing to Jesus whatever the church later said about him. It keeps to the contours of the way Jesus really spoke about himself, but goes, as it were, further in the direction Jesus indicated, in order to explain what it meant for Jesus to be 'the Son' of his divine Father and for Jesus to speak and act for God.

John's account of Jesus as the unique Son of God is particularly full and interesting. As in the Parable of the Vineyard in the Synoptic Gospels, Jesus in John is the Son sent by his Father to the people of Israel with full authority to act on God's behalf. When Jesus claims to be exercising the prerogatives of God, his opponents jump to the conclusion that he is making himself equal with God. But Jesus explains that he is not competing with God. He is the Son who can do what his Father does because he knows the Father and comes from the Father, but he acts only on the Father's initiative. He is the obedient Son to whom the Father has entrusted all his authority. There is no doubt that in John's Gospel, Jesus is no mere human son of the divine Father, but the eternal Son who has taken on human identity in order to give eternal life to the world. Yet it is through his self-denying obedience to God that Jesus fulfils his identity as the divine Son.

John's Gospel attributes to Jesus two rather different sets of 'I am' sayings. One is a set of figurative sayings in which Jesus makes such claims as 'I am the good shepherd' or 'I am the true vine'. These have a certain resemblance to the parables in the Synoptic Gospels in which Jesus characterizes the kingdom of God. In John, it is as though Jesus identifies himself with the key characters in parables. The effect is to portray Jesus as the one who gives eternal life (John's equivalent to 'the kingdom of God') in a variety of figurative expressions for this many-sided notion. In the Parable of the Shepherd that Jesus tells in Matthew's and Luke's Gospels, it is presumably God who is represented as the shepherd of the flock, but even in those Gospels it is Jesus who actually seeks and finds the lost sheep in his ministry. In John,

9. **Jesus as the Good Shepherd (catacomb fresco)**

Jesus himself is the shepherd who devotes himself to the flock even to the point of laying down his life for them. In Matthew's Gospel, Jesus speaks of the difficult way that leads to life, meaning the path he lays down for people to follow. In John's Gospel, Jesus is himself 'the way, the truth and the life'. Even in the Synoptics, Jesus is the indispensable agent of God's rule; in the figurative 'I am' sayings of John's Gospel, this is made much more explicit.

Could Jesus act with fully divine authority and exercise the divine prerogative of giving life, while being himself no more than a human servant of God? No, because in Jewish theology such prerogatives belong uniquely to God and cannot simply be delegated to someone else. They help to define who God is. Hence, even in the Synoptic Gospels, Jesus' claims to divine authority – to forgive sins or to share God's universal sovereignty – are regarded as blasphemy by Pharisees and chief priests. In John, the second set of 'I am' sayings is especially designed to indicate the personal identification of Jesus with God. In these sayings, Jesus says, in Greek, simply 'I am', though in English we must say 'I am he'. The words echo a formula that in the Hebrew Bible functions as the one God's declaration of his unique identity. Because God is utterly unique, not one of a kind of thing, God can identify himself only as the one he is: 'I am he'. That Jesus in John's Gospel makes the same declaration, sometimes rather ambiguously, but sometimes quite unambiguously, indicates his participation in God's own unique identity.

Many modern readers of the Gospels gain the impression that John has turned the merely human prophet of the three Synoptics into the figure Christians worship as God incarnate in human life. This contrast is certainly too stark. It cannot survive a more careful and nuanced appreciation of the way Jesus is portrayed in the Synoptic Gospels. The only Jesus we can plausibly find in the sources is a Jesus who, though usually reticent about it, speaks and acts for God in a way that far surpassed the authority of a prophet in the Jewish tradition. His opponents recognized this. Probably a lifetime of pondering it led to John's theologically creative interpretation of it. To do his Gospel justice, we must see that he is engaged, not in free creation, but in creative *interpretation* of the same Jesus the other Gospels, in their more restrained ways, also interpret.

Chapter 7
Death and a new beginning

Probably the best-known historical fact about Jesus is that he died on a Roman cross. In the modern world, the cross has long been Christianity's logo. For many people, it no longer evokes a form of judicial execution that in the ancient world was not only the most painful way to die (in reality a form of torture) but also the last word in social rejection and shame. The Romans did not invent crucifixion, but they made it an essential means of retaining power and maintaining order in their empire. The victim's slow death from exposure and asphyxiation was deliberately situated in a very public place so that it should act as a dramatic form of deterrence. Not justice but deterrence was the object, legitimating the most barbarous forms of cruelty as Roman soldiers amused themselves varying the details of the process of crucifixion. The better to shame the victim, onlookers were encouraged to taunt and jeer, as they do in the Gospel accounts about Jesus. It was a form of death reserved largely for slaves and rebels, for those who challenged the social and political order. Sometimes, as in Jesus' case, the victim's name and crime were placarded on the cross so that other would-be rebels might take note. Although many thousands of people suffered crucifixion, the accounts of Jesus' execution in the four Gospels, relatively lacking in detail though they are, are among the few extended accounts of crucifixion in ancient literature. Everyone knew how barbaric the process was, but the cultured elite preferred not to dwell on the fact that the much-vaunted peace and prosperity Rome gave to its empire required so much sadistic violence to maintain them. But in any case, only the dregs of the human race, people who did not matter, suffered crucifixion. Why should anyone bother to record their fate?

That the early Christians worshipped a crucified man was seen by their contemporaries as extraordinary. The apostle Paul said that

10. 'Alexamenos worships his God' (graffito from Rome, c. AD 200, mocking Christianity)

the crucified Messiah was 'a stumbling-block to Jews and foolishness to Gentiles' (1 Corinthians 1:23). For Jews, the Messiah was supposed to defeat the Romans, not fall victim to their violence, while for non-Jews crucifixion defined Jesus as a contemptible outcast. Their attitude is vividly illustrated by a crude graffito scratched on a wall in Rome around AD 200. A man raises his hand in prayer to a crucified figure with the head of a donkey, and the caption reads: 'Alexamenos worships his god'. Ludicrous as it seemed to many, the early Christians made no attempt to disguise the fact that they claimed for a crucified man the uniquely highest place in the cosmos. Not surprisingly, they were often regarded as a dangerously subversive movement.

The notice on Jesus' cross read: 'Jesus of Nazareth, the King of the Jews'. Clearly, it was as a rebel leader challenging the authority of Rome that he was executed. But what sort of threat to the Roman political order could Jesus have been supposed to be? We should avoid at once the idea that the criminal charge was mistaken because Jesus was a religious, not a political figure. Religion and politics were simply not separable in the way that claim supposes. In what follows, we shall try first to understand why Jesus' enemies thought him dangerous enough to be executed, and then consider how Jesus himself approached his death.

What led to Jesus' death?

There is no doubt that Jesus made enemies. In his native Galilee, the ruler Herod Antipas evidently considered him a dangerous troublemaker, too much like a successor to John the Baptist, whom Antipas had put to death. When Jesus travelled north of Galilee, to predominantly non-Jewish areas, it may well be that he was on the run from Antipas' men. He also antagonized many of the Pharisees. That he and they differed profoundly on matters of interpretation of Torah would not in itself have been a reason for them to seek his death, but the fact that he seemed to arrogate to himself uniquely divine authority could have put him into the category of a teacher who led the people into apostasy. Such an offence carried the penalty of death by stoning, a fate that Jesus narrowly escaped more than once. Common enemies make strange alliances, and it seems that Galilean Pharisees and supporters of Herod Antipas, who had different reasons for thinking Jesus dangerous, got together to plot his arrest. In the end, however, these Galilean opponents had little if anything to do with his death. It was events in Jerusalem that sealed his fate.

Whereas in Galilee Antipas held power as Rome's client ruler, in Jerusalem the Roman governor, Pontius Pilate, governed in collaboration with the local elite whose power base was the Temple. These were the high priest and his council, consisting of the chief priests (other members of the priestly aristocracy) and the heads of other aristocratic families. The council included a minority of Pharisees, not the sort of Pharisees Jesus encountered in Galilee, but wealthy aristocrats whom the Sadducean chief priests could not entirely exclude from power. John's Gospel, with its strong Jerusalem focus, sometimes refers to the ruling elite as 'the chief priests and the Pharisees', sometimes simply as 'the Jews', meaning the Jewish authorities who ran the Jewish Temple state. According to John's Gospel it was not at the end of his career that Jesus first clashed with these powerful people, but near the beginning. Their disputes escalated through a number of periods, short and long, that Jesus spent in Jerusalem. On the last such occasion before his final visit to Jerusalem, Jesus narrowly evaded arrest, and from then onwards it was clear that to go to Jerusalem would be to walk into the hands of authorities who had the will and the power to have him executed.

The deepest reason for conflict was that by claiming unparalleled authority to speak and act on God's behalf, Jesus challenged the right of the Temple elite to rule in God's name. But what precipitated the events that led directly to his death was the popularity of Jesus with the people, not only in Galilee but also in the Jerusalem area. The chief priests feared a popular uprising which the Romans would crush but which would cost them their own power. The danger of revolt was often in the air and never more so than at Passover time, when Jerusalem filled up with excitable pilgrims only too ready to envisage a new exodus event of liberation from Roman oppression. It was a week before Passover that Jesus rode into Jerusalem on a donkey and was hailed as Messiah by the crowds. The chief priests may well have realized that Jesus himself did not intend armed revolt. But this need not prevent him being the spark that ignited an uprising. They had to act quickly but also circumspectly. Fortunately for them, Judas Iscariot, one of Jesus' closest disciples, had evidently become deeply disillusioned by Jesus' failure to be the sort of Messiah he had expected. Judas provided the intelligence the chief priests needed in order to seize Jesus and deal with him before the crowds became aware of what was happening.

Of course, the chief priests could not simply assassinate Jesus. They had to administer the law. But neither could they themselves execute Jesus, even by due legal process, because administering the death penalty was one power that the Romans did not delegate to them. So they needed both to convict Jesus of a capital offence in Jewish law and also to persuade Pilate that the charge was one that he needed to take seriously. If they could get Jesus to admit to claiming to be the Messiah, this would probably take care of the latter requirement. In Roman terms, Messiah meant 'king of the Jews', making Jesus a rebel against Caesar. But it is doubtful whether claiming to be the Messiah could have been construed as a capital crime in Jewish law. After all, how could they prove that he was not in fact the Messiah? But Jesus eventually played into their hands. Asked by the high priest whether he was the Messiah, Jesus provided an answer that both incriminated him in the eyes of the assembled Jewish council members and could be represented to Pilate as a direct challenge to Roman rule. As we noticed in the last chapter, Jesus seems to have answered the direct question rather obliquely, as was his manner ('You say that I am'), but what he then added was altogether unequivocal: 'You will see the Son of man [in context obviously Jesus himself] seated at the right hand of the Power and coming on the clouds of heaven' (Mark 14:62). Such an identification of himself with God's unique sovereignty was blasphemy (as simply claiming to be the Messiah would not have been). Moreover, this explicit self-incrimination by Jesus dispensed with the need for witnesses, which had proved a difficulty in the unusual circumstances of legal proceedings held at night under pressure of time. It was essential to have Jesus dealt with before the onset of Passover.

Pilate, a shrewd politician who cared for little except his own career, seems to have decided that Jesus was harmless and was prepared to have him flogged and then to release him, expecting this would win him favour with the ordinary people. But the chief priests outmanoeuvred him, insisting that he could not be seen to deal leniently with a rebel against the empire. So it was that Jesus died as 'the king of the Jews' on a Roman cross.

Jesus and his death

From a quite early stage of his ministry, Jesus evidently expected a violent death. The best evidence is not the very explicit predictions (which might be suspected of being written after the event), but the figurative or enigmatic references, those that pose a riddle of the kind Jesus was in the habit of posing when he talked about his identity or his mission: 'the bridegroom will be taken away', 'I have a baptism with which to be baptized', 'You will search for me, but you will not find me'. Of course, it would not have been difficult for Jesus to foresee a violent end awaiting him. There was the disturbing precedent of John the Baptist, executed by Herod Antipas. Moreover, the messengers God sent to his people in the past had often been rejected and murdered, according to the Hebrew Bible and Jewish legends. In Jesus' parable of the Vineyard, he told a story in which the tenants of God's vineyard murdered a series of agents sent by the absentee landlord. The series culminated in the owner's own son, who was also killed. Jesus might, of course, have counted on divine providence to protect him, especially since there were attempts on his life that he escaped. But it is clear he did not. In fact, the opposite was the case: Jesus saw his death as the destiny his Father intended for him.

Jesus did more than expect his death; he also gave meaning to it. He spoke of it as a necessity, a divine 'must', and he found it written in Scripture. We have no good evidence that any other Jews of this period or earlier expected that the Messiah was to suffer and die. But, as we have observed already, the kind of role people attributed to the Messiah depended on which passages of the Hebrew Bible they chose to highlight. In Jesus' case, one of the scriptural passages in which he found himself was Isaiah's enigmatic narrative of the Servant of the Lord who bore the sins of his people and died as a sacrifice for them (Isaiah 52:15–53:12). Many scholars deny that Jesus' sayings make any reference to this passage, but the convincing evidence is the phrase 'for many' that recurs, as we shall see, in the two key sayings of Jesus about his death. Alluding to a passage of Scripture by means of a key catchphrase (in this case taken from Isaiah 53:12) was a feature of Jewish use of the Hebrew Bible.

Jesus saw his coming death as his final act of costly self-giving for others, the culmination of his whole career of embodying the compassionate love of God in order to bring forgiveness and healing into people's lives. 'The Son of man', he said, 'came not to be served but to serve, and to give his life a ransom for many' (Mark 10:45). The word 'ransom' (that is, the price of ransoming someone) recalls the Exodus, for according to the Hebrew Bible, Israel in Egypt were in a state of slavery from which God 'ransomed' them, that is, he bought their freedom and made them his people. The Passover lamb, slain on the night of the Exodus and subsequently at every annual Passover festival, could be seen as the 'price' by which God bought their liberty. Jesus here sees himself as the Passover lamb of the new exodus, offering his life as the ransom for his people, and at the same time as Isaiah's Servant of the Lord, who was 'like a lamb led to slaughter' when he sacrificed his life 'for many'.

Jesus celebrated Passover with his disciples the evening before he died. At the beginning of the meal, he did as every Jewish host did: he broke the loaf of bread into pieces and gave a piece to each of those present. Later, he took a cup of wine and passed it round for each to drink. But he gave these actions a startlingly new meaning. Of the bread, he said, 'Take; this is my body', and of the wine, 'This is my blood of the covenant which is poured out for many' (other versions have 'the new covenant'). This is sacrificial language (for the blood of an animal sacrifice in the Temple to be effective, the blood had to be poured out), as well as echoing Isaiah's Servant, who 'poured out himself to death'. But in offering the wine to be drunk, Jesus forges a strange new symbol. While the meat of a sacrificial animal would often be eaten, the blood would never be drunk. Jews were absolutely forbidden to consume blood, which was the God-given life of the animal. There must have been an element of shock in this extraordinary way of figuring Jesus' approaching death.

The connection of his blood with 'the (new) covenant' is another aspect of the Exodus theme. After the Exodus, God made Israel his own people by making a covenant with them, and the covenant was sealed with the blood of sacrificed oxen, called 'the blood of the covenant'. In the book of Jeremiah the prophet, God promised 'a new covenant', one that would transcend the people's disobedience to the first covenant. We can see in this allusion that Jesus saw his death as completing his mission to 'renew' the people of God, to make them the people of God's coming kingdom. As always, those who sat at table with him were the nucleus of this renewed Israel, but Jesus' sacrifice of himself was not for them only, but 'for many'. In facing rejection by the leaders of his people and death at their hands, Jesus has not at all given up hope for the success of his mission. On the contrary, the apparent failure he now faced was the paradoxical key to genuine success. (The word 'many' does not put a limit on the number envisaged. It means, not 'many' as opposed to 'all', but 'many' as opposed to 'one'. The one man Jesus poured out his life for the many.)

Soon after the Last Supper, in the Garden of Gethsemane, where Judas and the Temple police would soon arrive to arrest him, Jesus agonized over his coming death, begging the Father to spare him, but at the same time accepting it as his Father's will. This was surely more than an ordinary fear of death. What Jesus was now undertaking was a journey to the darkest extremity of the human condition, where, deserted by friends, mocked by enemies, left to an excruciatingly painful death, Jesus felt, like so many people suffering in extremity, that even God had abandoned him. According to Mark's Gospel, in his dying moments, Jesus summoned all his remaining strength in order to cry out, 'My God, my God, why have you abandoned me?' These are the words of a psalm that Jesus would certainly have known well, but he did not

11. **Ancient olive grove in Gethsemane**

speak them in Hebrew, as he would have done in regular prayer. He spoke them in his native Aramaic, making them utterly his own. They must have come to mind often in the preceding hours. Jesus knew that he, the one who was pouring himself out to death for the many, had for their sake to suffer the absence of God that the psalmist and many like him had known. Even this final agony was not private, but his final act of self-giving for others.

A new beginning?

At the point of Jesus' death on the cross, Mark's Gospel introduces some new characters who then become the central characters in the rest of this Gospel's narrative. They are the women disciples of Jesus, who, like the male disciples, had accompanied Jesus from Galilee, but whom Mark had not had occasion to mention until now. By this time, the male disciples were presumably in hiding, fearing for their own lives, but the women gathered to watch as Jesus died. Probably it was safer for them. Among a large number of women, Mark names three: Mary Magdalene, Mary the mother of James and Joses, and Salome. When Jesus is subsequently buried in a rock-hewn tomb, Mark notes that two of these women (the two Marys) are there, observing. It was the custom for women to perform the burial rites and so, after a Sabbath when no work could be done, the three women Mark has named go to the tomb with spices to anoint the body. They find the stone rolled away and the body missing. An angel tells them Jesus has been raised from death.

An interesting feature of this story is that the women are clearly portrayed as eyewitnesses. They watch and observe and see. This is almost all that they do. Moreover, Mark is very careful not to claim more than he knew was the case: only two of the named women observed his burial, while all three found the tomb empty. Obviously, he notes that two of them observed the burial so that readers may be assured that the women knew both that Jesus was buried and where. There was no mistake involved when they reported the body gone from the tomb. Mark knows that this crucial part of his narrative requires eyewitness testimony if it is to be believed, and he rather carefully provides it. The women were probably quite widely known in the early Christian communities, and Mark would certainly not have been the only one to have heard their story. The somewhat varying versions of the same story in all three of the other Gospels probably vary because they go back to different members of the group of women, who remembered somewhat differently, as people do.

But these eyewitnesses were women! As almost every scholar notes, in that society women were not trusted to give evidence. They were thought to be more emotional than men, and especially in religious matters apt to be credulous, too easily swayed by emotion. Celsus, a 2nd-century intellectual despiser of Christianity, dismissed the alleged testimony of Mary Magdalene by calling her 'a hysterical female'. Luke's Gospel candidly admits that at first even the male disciples did not believe these women's report. Not only were women unreliable; it was unsuitable that

12. Ancient Jewish tomb like the tomb of Jesus

women should be the first recipients of what was, in effect, a divine revelation. If Jesus had risen from death, the men ought to have been the first to know.

All this suggests that the stories were not simply invented. But before we consider what to make of them, we must take note of the reports in the Gospels and elsewhere that many people saw Jesus alive after his death. They recognized him (though not always at once), had conversations with him and even shared meals with him. All the Gospels except Mark tell at least two of these stories of Jesus' 'appearances', but it is evident that there were quite a lot of such stories from which the Gospel writers chose a few. In fact, the earliest account of them comes from Paul, writing in the year AD 52 or 53. He reproduces an established list which he had received from the Jerusalem apostles and which lists Jesus' appearances after his death to the following: Cephas (that is, Simon Peter, the leading member of the twelve), the twelve, five hundred believers at the same time (most of whom, Paul notes, were still alive when he was writing), James (Jesus' brother, who became a leading figure in the early Christian movement), 'all the apostles' (a larger category than the twelve), and finally Paul himself. Paul, who admits that his own encounter with the risen Christ was somewhat anomalous, had added himself to a traditional list.

It is noteworthy that Paul treats most of these people as people who were alive and known in the early Christian communities. They were still telling their own stories and anyone could consult them. The kind of evidence Paul offers is the personal testimony of many specific people who each had a story to tell – not, of course, of some neutrally observable fact, but of something extraordinary that happened to them and turned their lives around. These were people still living out of the events to which they testified.

It is worth considering just what the early Christians thought was happening in these experiences. First, it is very clear that they did not think that what people saw was the spirit of Jesus, surviving his physical death. They knew about ghosts and about dead people appearing in visions. If this had been the case with Jesus, it would have been very much less momentous than the 'resurrection' they believed had happened. The reports about the empty tomb fitted harmoniously with the appearance narratives, because the one who appeared was identified as Jesus in his whole bodily-spiritual identity. Jesus was not a soul who had left his body behind in the tomb. But, secondly, they did not think that Jesus had been resuscitated, like the dead people Jesus himself was reported to have brought back to life. Those people, such as the son of the widow of Nain, simply returned to this mortal life, very much like people resuscitated after 'clinical death' in modern hospitals. But Jesus was not like that. He appeared to people at will, and they do not seem to have wondered where he was when he was not making one of these relatively few appearances. While he took part, fleetingly, in ordinary human situations, he was evidently different. They believed he was raised to a new sort of bodily life, eternal life.

Such a notion of transformed bodily existence was certainly not unknown to Jews of the time, who called it resurrection. God, it was widely believed, was going to raise all the dead to new life at the end of history, when God abolishes evil and death and renews his whole creation. The first Christians thought that was what had happened to Jesus – but with the extraordinary qualification that it had happened to Jesus already, ahead of everyone else. There was no precedent in the Jewish tradition for claiming that this had happened to anyone else. It could have been nothing but a quite exotic surprise. When the early Christians assimilated this surprise, it came to form another bit of the picture Jesus himself had sketched of the kingdom of God arriving already, here and now, though not yet in its fullness. But all through early Christian literature runs the continuing sense of something that could never be seen as a matter of course, that was a source of irrepressible amazement.

To agree with the early Christians about what happened to Jesus requires taking on at least something of their wider religious worldview, as Christians do. Otherwise, one can perhaps get no further than saying that something entirely extraordinary must have happened for Jesus' disciples, left deeply disillusioned by Jesus' death, to come to believe that God had raised him from death. As the Japanese novelist Shusaku Endo puts it, in his *Life of Jesus* (1978), if we do not believe in the resurrection of Jesus, then 'we are forced to believe that what did hit the disciples was some other amazing event different in kind yet of equal force in its electrifying intensity'.

About a century after the death of Jesus, Rabbi Aqiva (Akiba) also suffered death at the hands of the Roman government, though the circumstances are obscure. What was remembered was that, under torture, he continued to recite the *Shema*, the Jewish confession of faith in the one and only God of Israel, until he died. He was one of the leading teachers of the early rabbinic movement. His interpretations of Torah were remembered and transmitted by his disciples. Had Jesus been no more than a teacher of Torah, he might have been remembered in the same way. His disciples would have honoured his memory and passed on his teaching. But Jesus was far from merely a teacher of Torah. He claimed God's authority to enact the arrival of God's kingdom. His disciples thought he was the Messiah, and he didn't deny being something of the sort. After his death, the disciples became much more confident that he really was the Messiah, because God had vindicated him, raised him from death and exalted him to sit on the divine throne in heaven. A remarkably new religious movement arose, first within Judaism, then of wider scope, that was based around the confidence that Jesus was the Messiah and was alive and active in the lives of those who followed him.

Rabbi Aqiva was remembered as having supported the claim of Simon bar Kokhba to be the Messiah. Bar Kokhba led the second major Jewish revolt against Rome (AD 132–135), but the revolt was crushed and Bar Kokhba died, presumably in the great battle that ended his messianic career. He was remembered in Jewish tradition only as a messianic pretender who failed, and Aqiva was remembered as foolish for having supported him. Had Jesus' story ended with his death on the cross, he too would have been remembered only as a failed would-be Messiah. Without some sort of a new beginning, whatever it might have been, there would have been no Christian faith and no Christian movement.

The Gospels, of course, were written from the perspective of Christian faith in the resurrection of Jesus and in order to encourage and inform faith in Jesus the risen and living Lord. For some readers, this may render them suspicious as sources for the history of Jesus. We might suspect them of projecting back into their accounts of the ministry of Jesus what Christians later came to believe about Jesus. But it is not unusual to interpret historical events from the perspective of their outcomes. In fact, this is what history, as distinct from chronicles, usually does. The Gospel writers believed that the Jesus whose story they told was known to Christian faith as the risen Lord, but they nevertheless evince a real sense of the pastness of the story they tell. Even the Gospel of John, which has most often been regarded as a story of the risen Christ with only the outward appearance of Jesus' earthly history, can on occasions explicitly point out the difference between what Jesus' disciples thought at the time and what they only came to understand later, after his resurrection. The early Christians believed that the risen Lord *was* Jesus of Nazareth. Only through faithful telling of the earthly history of Jesus up to his death could they know at all adequately who the presently living Christ was. They had good reason to preserve the stories and sayings from which they composed their Gospels.

Chapter 8
Jesus in Christian faith

The first Christians (though the term was not yet used) were all Jews and a large number of them formed a community in Jerusalem. Many of them, of course, had been disciples of Jesus before his death. Many had witnessed his appearances after his resurrection. They all believed that God had raised Jesus from death and had exalted him to heaven to share the divine throne from which God rules the universe. In the future, they believed, he would return to consummate the kingdom of God on earth. Meantime, he was the living focus of their lives and their worship. In place of his physical presence, he had sent the Spirit of God to be among them. They themselves were the renewed Israel, the messianic people of God, charged with continuing his mission.

It is important to realize that there was never a time, after the death of Jesus, when his followers regarded him simply as a teacher who had died a martyr's death and left them his teaching to live by. From the 19th century onwards, there have been recurrent attempts to cast the apostle Paul in the role of founder of Christianity. Paul, it is suggested, was the first to make Jesus the object of faith and worship. But all such theories founder on the fact that, apart from anything else, Paul did not have sufficient power and influence to invent Christianity. After coming to believe in Jesus the Messiah, Paul was a major Christian missionary, who did much to spread the Christian Gospel, especially among non-Jews, in the areas of modern Turkey and Greece. But there was already a large Christian community in Rome long before Paul visited the capital. Christianity must soon have spread to Egypt and to Mesopotamia, developments with which Paul had no involvement. Because the second half of the Acts of the Apostles, the only narrative we have of the early spread of Christianity, focuses on Paul's missionary travels, it is easy to get an exaggerated sense of their scope. Paul's letters, also preserved in the New Testament, are among the most impressive early expositions of Christian faith and influenced the later church immeasurably, but it was several decades before they circulated outside the churches Paul himself founded. The centre from which the early Christian movement developed and spread throughout the ancient world was not Paul, but the Jerusalem church, led initially by the twelve apostles and subsequently by James the brother of Jesus. What was common to the whole Christian movement derived from Jerusalem, not from Paul, and Paul himself derived the central message he preached from the Jerusalem apostles. The heart of Paul's teaching was common early Christian faith, though he was undoubtedly a thinker of genius who shaped that faith into a characteristic form, as did a number of other major teachers in the early church (such as the author of John's Gospel).

It was not Paul who made Jesus the object of Christian faith and worship. He is this in a variety of early Christian writings that were not influenced by Paul. Already, in the early Jerusalem community, Jesus was understood to be a living agent, not just a figure of the past. Though they continued to participate faithfully in the worship in the Temple in Jerusalem, these early believers also met to 'break bread', which meant to continue the table fellowship with Jesus that his disciples had enjoyed during his lifetime. Here his sacrificial death was remembered and appropriated. Here, he was addressed in prayer and even worshipped. This was an extraordinary development in a thoroughly Jewish context, for it was the first principle of Jewish faith that only the one God may be worshipped. Many scholars are therefore reluctant to conclude that the earliest Christians worshipped Jesus. But it was an understandable consequence of their belief that Jesus now sat at the right hand of God on the heavenly throne. This made him a participant in God's own unique sovereignty over his creation. Worship of God the only ruler of all things could now include worship of Jesus who shared that rule.

This is not the place for a full account of early Christian faith in Jesus, but enough has been said to show that, from the beginning, Jesus became integral to the version of Jewish monotheism that early Christianity was. No mere teacher or prophet, Jesus the living person was the one through whom God's universal kingdom was coming. Conversely, the whole of the early Christians' relationship with God was now mediated by Jesus. To have faith in Jesus was to have faith in God. To obey Jesus was to obey God. To hope for the coming of God to establish his kingdom in its fullness was to hope for the coming of Jesus. But, above all, to know God now was to know him as the Father of Jesus. Jesus' own prayers had been marked by his use of the Aramaic word 'Abba' as his constant form of address to God. Early Christians continued to use this word (so much so that in Paul's letters we find that the Aramaic word itself was still being used by Greek-speaking Christians who knew no Aramaic). The point was that Jesus opened up his own special and intimate relationship with the one he called Father for others to share. As adopted brothers and sisters of Jesus, they knew God as his and their Father.

That the faith of the early Christians focused on the living Jesus does not, of course, mean that they neglected the story of his life and death or the sayings that his disciples had learned. On the contrary, the stories and sayings were treasured and repeated, and only because they were so important at an early stage were they later given permanent written form in the Gospels. The stories portrayed the person who, in his heavenly glory, remained the same person. They portrayed the ways in which he continued to restore human life to wholeness, forgiving and healing all that was wrong. They also portrayed that way of relating to God as Abba that Jesus was drawing his followers into sharing. The teaching of Jesus informed and inspired them and challenged them to costly discipleship. The early Christians did not dissolve the past of Jesus into the present, but they remembered the earthly and crucified Jesus in order to know and to follow the living Christ.

It is not too much to say that the earliest Christians incorporated Jesus into their Jewish understanding of the one and only God. This was the origin of the doctrine of the incarnation, which in historic Christianity has been the central summary of the way Christians understand Jesus' relationship to humanity and to God. A brief explanation of the Christian doctrine of the incarnation will be an appropriate way to conclude this brief account of the place of Jesus in Christian faith. (The word 'incarnation', meaning enfleshment or embodiment, is based on the prologue to John's Gospel, which says that 'the Word became flesh'.)

The doctrine of the incarnation in its classic form is hardly separable from the doctrine of the Trinity, according to which God is believed to be a complex unity of three persons (acting subjects) in as intimate as possible a union. They are known as the Father, the Son, and the Holy Spirit. The names of the first two persons arise from taking the relationship of Jesus to God in the Gospels, a relationship of Son to Father, to reflect the eternal relationship of the Father and the Son within the Trinity. What happened in incarnation was that the Son became a human being, the 1st-century Jewish man Jesus.

The belief that Jesus was the divine person of the eternal Son become human does not make Jesus any the less human. The whole point of the doctrine is that the Son truly became a real human being. To grasp what is meant, one should first of all think of Jesus as a fully human person, human in his thoughts, his emotions, his physicality, his relationships. Jesus is as fully human as the rest of us (except that he did no wrong) and that full humanity is absolutely necessary for the doctrine of the incarnation. What the doctrine adds is that that human person was *God's* humanity. Uniquely in the case of this man, God actually lived a fully human life from birth to death. Moreover, it is important to realize Jesus never ceased to be human. In his resurrection and his heavenly glory, he models the destiny of all human beings.

The doctrine of the incarnation was never meant to take believers away from the concrete particularities of the Gospels into a realm of abstract doctrine. Rather, it is a sort of guide to reading the Gospels. It means that in the Jesus of the Gospels Christians find God revealed as never before or since. They find in the story of Jesus God's loving solidarity with all humanity. They find God identifying with humanity, even to the extent of suffering the extremity of pain, rejection, and degradation on Jesus' cross and dying his abandoned death. Incarnation means that God has shared in the human plight even at its most extreme in order that he might deliver people from that plight. The Gospels read as narratives of incarnation are at the heart of historic Christian faith.

Further reading

The approach to the nature of the four Gospels that I take in this book is further explained and justified in my *Jesus and the Eyewitnesses: The Gospels as Eyewitness Testimony* (Grand Rapids: Eerdmans, 2006), while the view of the early Christians' understanding of Jesus (Christology) that I take in Chapter 8 is based on my *Jesus and the God of Israel: God Crucified and Other Studies on the New Testament's Christology of Divine Identity* (Milton Keynes: Paternoster; Grand Rapids: Eerdmans, 2008).

A useful introduction to the range of views about the historical Jesus among current scholars is *The Historical Jesus: Five Views*, edited by James K. Beilby and Paul Rhodes Eddy (Downers Grove: InterVarsity Press, 2009; London: SPCK, 2010). James D. G. Dunn, John Dominic Crossan, Darrell L. Bock, Luke Timothy Johnson, and Robert M. Price each set out their own approach and also comment on the others'. A good textbook-style treatment, located in the scholarly mainstream, is Gerd Theissen and Annette Merz, *The Historical Jesus: A Comprehensive Guide*, translated by John Bowden (London: SCM Press, 1998). A variety of big books about the historical Jesus have been published in recent years: John Dominic Crossan, *The Historical Jesus: The Life of a Mediterranean Jewish Peasant* (Edinburgh: T. & T. Clark, 1991); N. T. Wright, *Jesus and the Victory of God* (London: SPCK, 1996); James D. G. Dunn, *Jesus Remembered* (Grand Rapids: Eerdmans, 2003); Craig S. Keener, *The Historical Jesus of the Gospels* (Grand Rapids: Eerdmans, 2009). Biggest of all is John

P. Meier, *A Marginal Jew: Rethinking the Historical Jesus* (New York: Doubleday, 1991–), of which four volumes have so far appeared: it is an exhaustive attempt to assess all the evidence using the standard tools of the 20th-century quest for the historical Jesus.

Shorter and more accessible treatments (ranging quite widely in their approaches) include E. P. Sanders, *The Historical Figure of Jesus* (London: Allen Lane [Penguin], 1993); Markus Bockmuehl, *This Jesus: Martyr, Lord, Messiah* (Edinburgh: T. & T. Clark, 1994); Geza Vermes, *The Religion of Jesus the Jew* (London: SCM Press, 1993); Marcus J. Borg, *Jesus: A New Vision*, 2nd edn. (New York: HarperCollins, 1991); Scot McKnight, *A New Vision for Israel* (Grand Rapids: Eerdmans, 1999); Marcus J. Borg and N. T. Wright, *The Meaning of Jesus: Two Visions* (San Francisco: HarperCollins, 1999); Joseph Ratzinger (Pope Benedict XVI), *Jesus of Nazareth*, tr. Adrian J. Walker (London: Bloomsbury, 2007) (the first of a two-volume work); Gerald O'Collins, *Jesus: A Portrait* (London: Darton, Longman & Todd, 2008).

Good defences of the historical reliability of the Gospels are Paul Rhodes Eddy and Gregory A. Boyd, *The Jesus Legend: A Case for the Historical Reliability of the Synoptic Jesus Tradition* (Grand Rapids: Baker Academic, 2007); and a pair of books by Paul W. Barnett: *Jesus and the Logic of History* (Leicester: Apollos, 1997) and *Finding the Historical Christ* (Grand Rapids: Eerdmans, 2009). The much more sceptical conclusions of the American scholars who make up the Jesus Seminar (conclusions reached by a process of voting) are best accessed in Robert W. Funk and Roy W. Hoover, *The Five Gospels: The Search for the Authentic Words of Jesus* (New York: Polebridge, 1993). A rare voice from the sceptical extreme is Robert M. Price, *The Incredible Shrinking Son of Man* (Amherst: Prometheus, 2003).

There are, of course, a very large number of books on particular aspects of Jesus' life and teaching. Among recent studies, the following are some of the most notable: Kenneth E. Bailey, *Jesus through Middle Eastern Eyes: Cultural Studies in the Gospels* (London: SPCK, 2008); Jonathan L. Reed, *Archaeology and the Galilean Jesus* (Harrisberg: Trinity Press International, 2000); Klyne Snodgrass, *Stories with Intent: A Comprehensive Guide to the Parables of Jesus* (Grand Rapids: Eerdmans, 2008); Richard A. Horsley, *Jesus and the Spiral of Violence: Popular Jewish Resistance in Roman Palestine* (Minneapolis: Fortress, 1993); Bruce Chilton, *Pure Kingdom: Jesus' Vision of God* (Grand Rapids: Eerdmans; London: SPCK, 1996); Richard Bauckham, *Gospel Women: Studies of the Named Women in the Gospels* (Grand Rapids: Eerdmans; Edinburgh: T. & T. Clark, 2002).

A useful reference book is the *Dictionary of Jesus and the Gospels*, edited by Joel B. Green, Scot McKnight, and I. Howard Marshall (Downers Grove/Leicester: InterVarsity Press, 1992). *The Cambridge Companion to Jesus*, edited by Markus Bockmuehl (Cambridge: Cambridge University Press, 2001) is a compendium of essays on a wide range of topics concerning Jesus. David F. Ford and Mike Higton (eds.), *Jesus* (Oxford: Oxford University Press, 2002) is a compendium of over 340 extracts of material about Jesus from 20 centuries.

There is a huge literature on the Gospels and commentaries on them. Two of the best general books are Martin Hengel, *The Four Gospels and the One Gospel of Jesus Christ*, tr. John Bowden (London: SCM Press, 2000); Markus Bockmuehl and Donald A. Hagner, *The Written Gospel* (Cambridge: Cambridge University Library, 2005). On Jesus in other sources, see Robert E. Van Voorst, *Jesus Outside the New Testament* (Grand Rapids: Eerdmans, 2000). On the Gnostic Gospels and their contemporary impact, see Philip Jenkins, *Hidden Gospels* (Oxford: Oxford University Press, 2001) and Darrell L. Bock, *The Missing Gospels* (Louisville: Thomas Nelson, 2006).

On Jesus in the faith of the early Christians, see Larry W. Hurtado, *Lord Jesus Christ: Devotion to Jesus in Earliest Christianity* (Grand Rapids: Eerdmans, 2003); Richard N. Longenecker (ed.), *Contours of Christology in the New Testament* (Grand Rapids: Eerdmans, 2005); Robert M. Bowman and J. Ed Komoszewski, *Putting Jesus in His Place: The Case for the Deity of Christ* (Grand Rapids: Kregel, 2007).

Beverly Roberts Gaventa and Richard B. Hays have edited the essays of a working group that, while taking full account of the historical quest for Jesus, takes account also of the church's tradition and the present reality of Jesus: *Seeking the Identity of Jesus: A Pilgrimage* (Grand Rapids: Eerdmans, 2008).

On Jesus in Christian theology, see Oliver D. Crisp, 'Incarnation', in *The Oxford Handbook of Systematic Theology*, ed. John Webster, Kathryn Tanner, and Iain Torrance (Oxford: Oxford University Press, 2007), pp. 160–75; Gerald O'Collins, *Christology: A Biblical, Historical and Systematic Study of Jesus* (Oxford: Oxford University Press, 1995); Stephen T. Davis, Daniel Kendall, and Gerald O'Collins (eds.), *The Incarnation: An Interdisciplinary Symposium on the Incarnation of the Son of God* (Oxford: Oxford University Press, 2002).

On Jesus in the history of culture, see Jaroslav Pelikan, *Jesus through the Centuries: His Place in the History of Culture* (New Haven/London: Yale University Press, 1985); Stephen Prothero, *American Jesus: How the Son of God Became a National Icon* (New York: Farrar, Straus & Giroux, 2003); Gabriele Finaldi, *The Image of Christ* (London: National Gallery Company, 2002).

On Jesus in other faiths, see Gregory A. Barker (ed.), *Jesus in the World's Faiths: Leading Thinkers from Five Religions Reflect on His Meaning* (New York: Orbis, 2007); Gregory A. Barker and Stephen E. Gregg (eds.), *Jesus Beyond Christianity: The Classic Texts* (Oxford: Oxford University Press, 2010); Tarif Khalidi, *The*

Muslim Jesus: Sayings and Stories in Islamic Literature
(Cambridge, Mass.: Harvard University Press, 2001).

In these recommendations, I have focused on the most recent
literature, not because it is necessarily the best, but because the
older literature can be accessed via the more recent.

Index

A

Abba 65–7, 86, 112–13
Abraham 21, 47, 67
actions, communication
     through 58
Acts of the Apostles 111
aphorisms 60–1, 68, 77
appearances of Jesus after
     death 106–7, 110
Aqiva, Rabbi, death of 108–9
Aramaic 65–6, 104, 112
authority of Jesus 84–6, 89–94,
     97–8, 108

B

baptism 33
Bartimaeus 47
beatitudes 78
beggars, healing 40–1, 49, 50
blasphemy 89, 93, 100
blood 102–3
burial of Jesus 104–7

C

Cana, wedding at 56
carpenter, Jesus as a 27–8
children 76, 77–8
Christian faith, Jesus in the 110–14

commandments 22, 26, 52, 64,
     68–72, 75, 80
common Judaism 20–3
compassion 42–3, 50–1, 54–6, 64,
     66, 82, 101
context 16–34
covenant relationship 66–7, 75,
     102–3
cross as symbol 95
crucifixion 31, 95–7,
     100, 109
culture 1–3

D

David, house of 30–1, 87
dead, raising the 42, 56, 107
Dead Sea Scrolls 16, 26, 30
death of Jesus 10, 87, 89, 95–111,
     114
debt and sin 82
demons, possession with 39–40,
     49, 50, 54, 84, 88
destruction, meaning of 81–3
disciples 33, 38, 50–4, 61–2, 66,
     73–6, 108–13
     number 51–2, 89–90
     women 51–2, 104–6
donkey, riding into Jerusalem
     on a 88, 99

E

education of Jesus 30
Endo, Shusaku 108
Essenes 24, 25–6, 27, 68, 73
eternal life 55–6, 107
ethics, Jesus as teacher of 15, 35, 45–6, 60, 69–73
evil 36, 39–41, 68, 71, 84, 107
Exodus 21, 27, 31, 51, 63, 86, 89–90, 101–2
exorcisms 39–40, 51, 54, 84, 88
'eye for an eye' 72
eyewitnesses 13–17, 104–6

F

faith 43, 109, 110–13
family 76, 80, 112
fasting 46
Father, God as 64–7, 75–6, 80, 86, 90–1, 112–13
feet, washing 58, 76–7
folklore 10–13
forgiveness 84–5, 101, 113
form-criticism 12–14
future, images of the 83

G

Galilee 17, 20, 27–30, 54, 97–8, 104
Gentiles 23, 49, 54, 62, 76, 79, 97, 111
Gnostic Gospels 7–10
Good Samaritan 70–1, 73
Gospels 4–17, 43, 65, 78, 112–14
   see also individual gospels
   appearances after death 106
   biography 8, 15, 47
   context 16–17
   dates 10
   death of Jesus 98, 103–6
   historical sources, as 5, 6–17
   identity of Jesus 87, 90–4
   literature, as 15
   Messianism 31, 87
   names 47
   narrative framework 7–9
   other gospels 7–10
   parables and aphorisms 59, 61
   poor 48–9
   resurrection 109
   Sermon on the Mount 74–5
   Synoptics 17, 35, 55, 59, 61, 90–1, 93
Greek 65–6, 84

H

healing 38–43, 46–51, 53, 55–6, 73, 87–8
Hegesippus 29
Herod Antipas 20, 29, 33, 45, 52, 58, 62, 97–8, 100
hierarchy 77–80
historical Jesus 5, 6–17
holiness 44–5, 62, 72
humanity 2–3, 55, 113–14
humility 77, 88–9

I

identity of Jesus 84–94
images of Jesus 4–5
immersion in water 23, 33
incarnation, doctrine of the 113–14
indirect communication 57–61
   see also parables
interiorization 70, 72
interpretation 6–7, 15–17, 24–6, 29–30, 68–75, 94, 97, 108–9
Isaac 47, 67
Isaiah 102

J

Jacob 47, 67
Jeremiah 75, 102
Jerusalem see also Temple in Jerusalem

Jesus

destruction 17, 27
donkey, riding into Jerusalem
    on a 88, 99
early Christian movement 47
final visit of Jesus 47, 51, 88,
    98–9
gospels 30
Passover 21, 110–11
Roman rule 18–19
Jewish parties 24–7, 34
Jewish teacher, Jesus as a 2, 9
Joanna 49, 52
John, Gospel of 10, 11, 17, 54–6, 61,
    93, 98, 109, 111, 113
John the Baptist 33–4, 41–2, 44,
    50, 85, 88, 90–4, 100
Joseph, father of Jesus 27, 29
Josephus 24, 26–7
Judaea 17, 18–19, 27
Judaism in 1st century
    Palestine 20–3
Judas, brother of Jesus 29
Judas Iscariot 99, 103
Judas the Galilean 26–7

K

king, God as 64, 75
kingdom of God
    Abba, the God of the
        kingdom 62–8
    children 77–8
    coming of the Kingdom 36–7,
        46, 53–4, 75, 85, 87, 107–8, 112
    enacting the 35–56
    exclusion 82
    John, Gospel of 54–6
    meaning 36
    metaphors and motifs 57, 59
    poor, belonging to the 47–50, 77–9
    table, enacting at 43–7
    teaching of kingdom of
        God 57–83
    timing 37
Kokhba, Simon bar 108–9

L

Last Judgment 90
Last Supper 102–3
lepers 40–1, 49
levites 70–1
'love thy enemy' 71–2, 80
'love thy neighbour' 69–71
Luke, Gospel of 10, 15, 51–2, 78, 87,
    105–6

M

Mark, Gospel of 10, 15, 16, 27–8,
    47, 65, 69, 87, 103–5
Mary and Martha 53
Mary Magdalene 52, 104–5
Matthew, Gospel of 10, 15, 27–8,
    74, 78, 87
Messianism 9, 30–2, 33, 41–2,
    46–7, 84, 86–91, 97, 99–101,
    108–11
metaphors and motifs 57–8
miracles 38–43, 46–51, 53–6, 73,
    84, 86–8, 107
monotheism 21–2, 112, 113
Moses 26, 31, 63, 66, 68–9, 71–2,
    86, 89–90

N

name of God 22, 63–4, 66–7
names 47–8, 63–4, 66–7
Nazareth 27–8, 76
Nicodemus 49, 55, 62

O

oath, lying on 72
oppression 2, 21–3, 37–8, 64, 76
oral tradition 10–14, 24, 61

P

Palestine in 1st Century 16–34,
    58–9
Papias, bishop of Hierapolis 15

parables 27–8, 30, 37, 58–60,
    64, 70–1, 73, 81–2,
    86, 90, 92–3
Passover 21, 99–102
Paul 65, 96–7, 106, 110–12
Peter 15, 16, 87, 106
Pharisees 24–5, 26, 27, 29–30, 34,
    44–6, 52, 68, 72–5, 93, 97–8
political and religious context 18–
    20
political issues 79–80
Pontius Pilate 18–19, 98–9
poor 47–51, 62, 76, 77–9
Prodigal Son 60
prophecies 22, 30–1, 33, 38, 42–3,
    63, 66, 75, 86, 88, 102
prostitutes 45, 46
purity 23, 25, 29, 41, 44–6, 54,
    70–3

R

ransom 101–2
religious context 18–20
renewal of the people of God 50–4
resurrection 8–9, 104–10, 114
retaliation 72
revolts against Rome 17, 26–7, 31,
    97–8, 108–9
riddles 58, 61, 100
Romans
  crucifixion 9
  death of Jesus 95–9
  enemy, loving your 72
  John the Baptist 33–4
  kingdom of God, coming of
    the 37–8, 80
  Messiah 31, 87
  Pharisees 25
  political and religious
    context 18–20
  revolts 17, 27, 108–9
  Sadducees 26
  tax 45
rule of God

arrival of 35–8, 53, 75–6
healing power 38–43, 46, 55–6
Temple theocracy 79–80

S

Sabbath, observance of the 73–4,
    104
sacrifice 21–2, 79, 102–3, 111
Sadducees 24, 26, 98
Samaritans 49, 62, 70–1, 73
sayings or aphorisms 10, 17, 30,
    101, 112
self-incrimination 99–100
Sepphoris 29, 62
Sermon on the Mount 74–5
Shema 69–70, 108
Shepherd, Parable of the 92–3
sin 23, 33, 44–6, 50, 82, 84–5, 93,
    101
sinners, Jesus befriending 44–6,
    50
slaves 76–7, 81–2, 86, 95, 101
social relationships 75–9
social status 77–80
Son of God, Jesus as 33, 90–4,
    100, 113–14
sources 5, 6–17
style of teaching 57–62
symbolism 21, 41, 44, 50, 55–6

T

tax and tax collectors 20, 21, 26,
    45–6, 49
teaching of kingdom of God 57–83
Temple in Jerusalem
  common identity 20
  destruction 17, 27
  early Christians 111
  pilgrimages 29–30
  presence of God 21, 36
  teaching in courts 62
  warning of divine
    judgment 82–3

Jesus

Ten Commandments 22, 26, 52, 64, 68–74, 80
theocracy 79–80
Thomas, Gospel of 9–10
Tiberias 29, 62
tomb of Jesus 104–7
Torah 21–2, 24–5, 45–6, 62, 68–75, 97, 108
traditions 10–14, 17, 68–9, 74–5, 107
Trinity, doctrine of the 113
twelve tribes of Israel 50–1, 89

U

universal icon, Jesus as 1–5
Unmerciful Servant, Parable of the 81–2

V

Vineyard, Parable of the 86, 90–1, 100–1

W

women 51–2, 62, 104–6

Y

YHWH 22, 63, 66–7

Z

Zacchaeus 45
Zealots 26
Zechariah 88

Expand your collection of
VERY SHORT INTRODUCTIONS

1. Classics
2. Music
3. Buddhism
4. Literary Theory
5. Hinduism
6. Psychology
7. Islam
8. Politics
9. Theology
10. Archaeology
11. Judaism
12. Sociology
13. The Koran
14. The Bible
15. Social and Cultural Anthropology
16. History
17. Roman Britain
18. The Anglo-Saxon Age
19. Medieval Britain
20. The Tudors
21. Stuart Britain
22. Eighteenth-Century Britain
23. Nineteenth-Century Britain
24. Twentieth-Century Britain
25. Heidegger
26. Ancient Philosophy
27. Socrates
28. Marx
29. Logic
30. Descartes
31. Machiavelli
32. Aristotle
33. Hume
34. Nietzsche
35. Darwin
36. The European Union
37. Gandhi
38. Augustine
39. Intelligence
40. Jung
41. Buddha
42. Paul
43. Continental Philosophy
44. Galileo
45. Freud
46. Wittgenstein
47. Indian Philosophy
48. Rousseau
49. Hegel
50. Kant
51. Cosmology
52. Drugs
53. Russian Literature
54. The French Revolution
55. Philosophy
56. Barthes
57. Animal Rights
58. Kierkegaard
59. Russell
60. Shakespeare
61. Clausewitz
62. Schopenhauer
63. The Russian Revolution
64. Hobbes
65. World Music

66. Mathematics
67. Philosophy of Science
68. Cryptography
69. Quantum Theory
70. Spinoza
71. Choice Theory
72. Architecture
73. Poststructuralism
74. Postmodernism
75. Democracy
76. Empire
77. Fascism
78. Terrorism
79. Plato
80. Ethics
81. Emotion
82. Northern Ireland
83. Art Theory
84. Locke
85. Modern Ireland
86. Globalization
87. The Cold War
88. The History of Astronomy
89. Schizophrenia
90. The Earth
91. Engels
92. British Politics
93. Linguistics
94. The Celts
95. Ideology
96. Prehistory
97. Political Philosophy
98. Postcolonialism
99. Atheism
100. Evolution
101. Molecules
102. Art History
103. Presocratic Philosophy
104. The Elements
105. Dada and Surrealism
106. Egyptian Myth
107. Christian Art
108. Capitalism
109. Particle Physics
110. Free Will
111. Myth
112. Ancient Egypt
113. Hieroglyphs
114. Medical Ethics
115. Kafka
116. Anarchism
117. Ancient Warfare
118. Global Warming
119. Christianity
120. Modern Art
121. Consciousness
122. Foucault
123. The Spanish Civil War
124. The Marquis de Sade
125. Habermas
126. Socialism
127. Dreaming
128. Dinosaurs
129. Renaissance Art
130. Buddhist Ethics
131. Tragedy
132. Sikhism
133. The History of Time
134. Nationalism
135. The World Trade Organization
136. Design
137. The Vikings
138. Fossils
139. Journalism

140. The Crusades
141. Feminism
142. Human Evolution
143. The Dead Sea Scrolls
144. The Brain
145. Global Catastrophes
146. Contemporary Art
147. Philosophy of Law
148. The Renaissance
149. Anglicanism
150. The Roman Empire
151. Photography
152. Psychiatry
153. Existentialism
154. The First World War
155. Fundamentalism
156. Economics
157. International Migration
158. Newton
159. Chaos
160. African History
161. Racism
162. Kabbalah
163. Human Rights
164. International Relations
165. The American Presidency
166. The Great Depression and The New Deal
167. Classical Mythology
168. The New Testament as Literature
169. American Political Parties and Elections
170. Bestsellers
171. Geopolitics
172. Antisemitism
173. Game Theory
174. HIV/AIDS
175. Documentary Film
176. Modern China
177. The Quakers
178. German Literature
179. Nuclear Weapons
180. Law
181. The Old Testament
182. Galaxies
183. Mormonism
184. Religion in America
185. Geography
186. The Meaning of Life
187. Sexuality
188. Nelson Mandela
189. Science and Religion
190. Relativity
191. The History of Medicine
192. Citizenship
193. The History of Life
194. Memory
195. Autism
196. Statistics
197. Scotland
198. Catholicism
199. The United Nations
200. Free Speech
201. The Apocryphal Gospels
202. Modern Japan
203. Lincoln
204. Superconductivity
205. Nothing
206. Biography
207. The Soviet Union
208. Writing and Script

209. Communism
210. Fashion
211. Forensic Science
212. Puritanism
213. The Reformation
214. Thomas Aquinas
215. Deserts
216. The Norman Conquest
217. Biblical Archaeology
218. The Reagan Revolution
219. The Book of Mormon
220. Islamic History
221. Privacy
222. Neoliberalism
223. Progressivism
224. Epidemiology
225. Information
226. The Laws of Thermodynamics
227. Innovation
228. Witchcraft
229. The New Testament
230. French Literature
231. Film Music
232. Druids
233. German Philosophy
234. Advertising
235. Forensic Psychology
236. Modernism
237. Leadership
238. Christian Ethics
239. Tocqueville
0. Landscapes and
   Geomorphology
   Spanish Literature

242. Diplomacy
243. North American Indians
244. The U.S. Congress
245. Romanticism
246. Utopianism
247. The Blues
248. Keynes
249. English Literature
250. Agnosticism
251. Aristocracy
252. Martin Luther
253. Michael Faraday
254. Planets
255. Pentecostalism
256. Humanism
257. Folk Music
258. Late Antiquity
259. Genius
260. Numbers
261. Muhammad
262. Beauty
263. Critical Theory
264. Organizations
265. Early Music
266. The Scientific Revolution
267. Cancer
268. Nuclear Power
269. Paganism
270. Risk
271. Science Fiction
272. Herodotus
273. Conscience
274. American Immigration
275. Jesus

THE BIBLE
A Very Short Introduction
John Riches

It is sometimes said that the Bible is one of the most unread books in the world, yet it has been a major force in the development of Western culture and continues to exert an enormous influence over many people's lives. This Very Short Introduction looks at the importance accorded to the Bible by different communities and cultures and attempts to explain why it has generated such a rich variety of uses and interpretations. It explores how the Bible was written, the development of the canon, the role of Biblical criticism, the appropriation of the Bible in high and popular culture, and its use for political ends.

'John Riches' clear and lively Very Short Introduction offers a distinctive approach to the Bible ... a distinguished addition to the series.'

Christopher Rowland, University of Oxford

'Short in length, but not in substance, nor in interest. A fascinating introduction both to the way in which the Bible came to be what it is, and to what it means and has meant for believers.'

Joel Marcus, Boston Univers

www.oup.com/vsi/